Success of any mission requires quality people at the appropriate place and time. Effective personnel support is, therefore, the linchpin for successful joint operations. Joint Publication (JP) 1-0, *Joint Personnel Support,* represents our commitment to this vital operational readiness component.

As the joint force continues to adapt to the changing security environment and evolves to meet the expectations of national leadership and the American public, JP 1-0 provides a baseline of validated procedures, processes, and systems to provide the flexibility, agility, and adaptability to meet the manpower and personnel requirements of the joint force. We must continue maturing our joint operating concepts. As such, evenly leveraging the talents of all individuals and their respective Services and components should be a primary consideration.

I urge each of you to read JP 1-0, use its principles as practitioners of joint doctrine, and ensure its widest dissemination.

MARTIN E. DEMPSEY
General, U.S. Army

PREFACE

1. Scope

This publication is the keystone document of the personnel series. It provides doctrine for planning, coordinating, and providing personnel support to joint operations.

2. Purpose

This publication has been prepared under the direction of the Chairman of the Joint Chiefs of Staff and sets forth joint personnel doctrine to govern the activities and performance of the Armed Forces of the United States in joint operations. It prescribes the joint doctrinal framework within which personnel support is provided for the total force and provides military guidance for use by the Armed Forces of the United States in preparing their appropriate personnel plans.

3. Application

a. Joint doctrine established in this publication applies to the Joint Staff, commanders of combatant commands, subunified commands, joint task forces, subordinate components of these commands, combat support agencies, and the Services.

b. The guidance in this publication is authoritative; as such, this doctrine will be followed except when, in the judgment of the commander, exceptional circumstances dictate otherwise. If conflicts arise between the contents of this publication and the contents of Service publications, this publication will take precedence unless the Chairman of the Joint Chiefs of Staff, normally in coordination with the other members of the Joint Chiefs of Staff, has provided more current and specific guidance. Commanders of forces operating as part of a multinational (alliance or coalition) military command should follow multinational doctrine and procedures ratified by the United States. For doctrine and procedures not ratified by the United States, commanders should evaluate and follow the multinational command's doctrine and procedures, where applicable and consistent with US law, regulations, and doctrine.

SUMMARY OF CHANGES
REVISION OF JOINT PUBLICATION 1-0
DATED 16 OCTOBER 2006

- **Renamed publication to *Joint Personnel Support***

- **Addresses the joint personnel visibility concept in basic publication**

- **Addresses Sexual Assault Prevention and Response Program in basic publication**

- **Addresses and updates postal support responsibilities and procedures**

- **Adds postal support to detainee operations**

- **Adds Appendix P, *Language and Regional Expertise Management***

- **Expands and further clarifies the Joint Individual Augmentee process in accordance with revised Chairman of the Joint Chiefs of Staff Instruction 1301.01**

- **Addresses the optional establishment of a joint personnel operations center within the manpower and personnel directorate of a joint staff at the combatant command level to facilitate the integration of personnel support to joint operations**

Intentionally Blank

TABLE OF CONTENTS

GLOSSARY

FIGURE

- **Discusses the Organization, Functions, and Principles of Personnel Support**

- **Describes Roles and Responsibilities for Personnel Support to Joint Operations**

- **Explains Joint Personnel Planning, Including Personnel Estimate, Joint Manning Document, and Global Force Management**

Organization, Functions, and Principles of Personnel Support

Personnel Services Support	Personnel services support is a sustainment function executed at the tactical, operational, and strategic levels by the Services under their Title 10, United States Code (USC), authority. Integrated personnel support is a vital component of operational effectiveness and, when executed properly, becomes a combat multiplier for the joint force. The joint force commander (JFC) and the manpower and personnel directorate of a joint staff (J-1) continually maintain visibility of personnel manning levels to anticipate requirements and provide timely manpower support to planned operations or to direct the planning and execution of branches or sequels that can best accomplish the task, given existing constraints and restraints.
Authorities	Authorization and guidance for implementation of personnel programs in support of joint operations are set forth in Titles 5, 10, 38, and 39, USC, and in Department of Defense (DOD) and Chairman of the Joint Chiefs of Staff (CJCS) issuances. Services and Service components will retain authority for personnel support to their forces assigned or attached to joint commands, subject to the coordinating guidance of the J-1 issued under the authority of the JFC.
Organization of the Joint Force Manpower and Personnel Directorate	The J-1 section of a joint force headquarters (HQ) may be organized under a director of manpower and personnel and may have the follow divisions:

- **Personnel readiness** provides plans, policy, and guidance on joint personnel issues, to include oversight of joint personnel operations.

- **Joint manpower** provides policy oversight on joint manpower and management of joint forces and US contributions to multinational military organizations.

- **Personnel services** administers internal staff, DOD civilian, and military members of the joint force. It also includes limited administrative requirements related to DOD contractors authorized to accompany the force (CAAF).

- **Director's action group,** when established, reviews policies pertaining to the separation/retirement of military personnel, concurrent receipt, survivor benefits, veterans' issues, assignment policy, force realignment and transformation, quality of life issues, compensation, and recruiting and retention.

Function of the Joint Force Manpower and Personnel Directorate

A joint force J-1's function is to enhance personnel readiness and operational capabilities of the joint force within its operational area. The J-1 is the focal point for joint manpower and personnel actions.

Principles of Personnel Support Within a Joint Force Command

Command Emphasis. Ensuring the proper planning and execution of personnel support activities is a JFC's responsibility and must receive high priority.

Synchronization of Personnel Support. The J-1 coordinates with other staff directorates and supported and supporting organizations to synchronize personnel support efforts for all possible operational requirements during every phase of the operation.

Unity of Effort. Timely and effective personnel support is accomplished through detailed J-1 planning and coordination. Integration involves joining all elements of personnel support and personnel service support (tasks, functions, systems, processes, and organizations) with operations ensuring unity of purpose and effort to accomplish the mission.

Flexibility and Responsiveness. The J-1 must be able to respond to changing situations, unanticipated events, and varying personnel-related requirements on short notice. Personnel support programs, policies, techniques, and procedures should be adaptable to shifting operational situations, needs, and priorities.

Roles and Responsibilities

Responsibilities of Secretary of Defense, Chairman of the Joint Chiefs of Staff, Military Department Secretaries, Service Chiefs, and Department of Defense Agencies

Secretary of Defense (SecDef) establishes policy, assigns responsibilities, and prescribes procedures for personnel readiness issues as they apply to the Active Component (AC) and Reserve Component (RC), DOD civilians, and US contractors. This includes the Joint Staff, DOD agencies, and Military Departments.

The **CJCS**, in consultation with the other members of the Joint Chiefs of Staff, advises SecDef on manpower and personnel issues impacting the readiness of the Armed Forces of the United States and the force structure required to support attainment of national security objectives.

Functions of the **Secretaries of the Military Departments** are outlined in the USC and are generally referred to as Title 10, USC, responsibilities. These responsibilities include the functions of recruiting, organizing, supplying, equipping, training, servicing, mobilizing, demobilizing, administering, and maintaining the Services.

DOD agencies formulate and publish policies and procedures outlining the requirement for their deployed, deploying, and redeploying personnel to adhere to the geographic combatant commander (GCC) guidance on entry/exit procedures.

Combatant Command Responsibilities

Combatant commanders (CCDRs) exercise combatant command (command authority) over assigned forces, which allows them to direct and approve those aspects of personnel support necessary to carry out assigned missions and to standardize personnel policies as they deem necessary. The CCDR establishes personnel policies to ensure proper and uniform standards of military conduct. The CCDR utilizes the manpower, workforce, and individual augmentation capabilities in the Electronic Joint Manpower and Personnel System (e-JMAPS) to provide visibility of personnel assigned.

Joint Force Command Manpower and Personnel Directorate Responsibilities

The J-1 is the principal staff officer for manpower management, personnel management, and personnel services support. The J-1 develops joint plans, policy, and guidance on manpower and personnel issues;

coordinates manpower and personnel support to facilitate the success of operations; maintains a dialogue with other staff directorates, Service components, and outside military and civilian agencies while also keeping subordinate commanders informed of personnel actions that affect their command and their Service members. The J-1 has primary responsibility for the following functions: personnel management; manpower management; personnel augmentation; joint personnel training and tracking activities; personnel accountability and strength reporting; rotation policies; civilian employees; pay and entitlements; postal operations; morale, welfare, and recreation; casualty operations and casualty reporting; and awards and decorations.

Service Component Responsibilities

Service components shall account for all personnel, including AC, RC, DOD civilians, and civilian contractors under their operational control. Accountability begins immediately upon personnel entering theater, to include short notice operations. In addition to recruiting, organizing, equipping, and training, the Services and their components have responsibility for providing personnel support to their forces. The Services retain administrative control and accountability responsibilities for their forces assigned and attached to combatant commands (CCMDs). United States Special Operations Command organizes, trains and equips its forces, but uses its coordinating authority to interact with the Services concerning personnel management of special operations forces.

Other Command and Component Responsibilities

The J-1 provides support and assistance to the office of primary responsibility on the following matters: RC call-up; stop-loss authority; noncombatant evacuation operations and noncombatant repatriation; personnel recovery operations; and detainee operations.

Other Operational Considerations

Although not applicable in all situations, the following issues should be considered when planning personnel support to joint operations. These include considerations on single-service manager, uniform policies; evaluation reports; passports and visas; personnel accountability in conjunction with natural or man-made disasters; multinational operations; and redeployment operations.

Joint Personnel Planning

Effective planning for personnel support to joint operations can support the ability of the combatant commander, joint force commander, and commander, joint task force, to accomplish the mission.

Joint personnel planning is the means by which the J-1 envisions the desired end state in support of the commander's mission requirements. Planning establishes the methods for understanding the situation and analyzing a mission; developing, analyzing, and comparing courses of action (COAs); selecting the most favorable COA; and producing the personnel annex for the command's plans and orders. The J-1 must be fully involved in all phases of deliberate planning and crisis action planning efforts and collaborate with other staff directors in the preparation of the commander's estimate, plan development, and force flow conferencing.

Personnel Estimate

The purpose of the personnel estimate is to collect and analyze relevant information for developing (within the time limits and available information) the most effective solution to a problem. The J-1 assists the commander in reaching a decision by estimating whether a particular operation or mission is supportable from a personnel perspective.

Joint Manning Document Development

Once a mission is delineated via SecDef orders, the unit identified to form the core of the joint task force (JTF) HQ must identify its personnel requirements. These requirements are translated into a joint manning document (JMD) to ensure adequate manning levels with a proper mix of military and civilian personnel with the correct skills to ensure mission success.

JTF Roles. The commander, joint task force (CJTF), in concert with the establishing commander's staff, develops and organizes a draft JTF JMD that will be forwarded for the establishing commander's validation and approval. During JMD development, the CJTF will evaluate current personnel resources available to meet requirements. The CJTF must seek to fill as many requirements as possible from CJTF's immediate available personnel assets consistent with mission requirements and guidelines for forming a JTF. The CCMD J-1 will attempt to fill any remaining vacancies in JMD billets from internal assets prior to requesting Joint Staff J-1 for joint individual augmentation (JIA) support.

Establishing CCDR Roles. If the establishing CCDR decides to direct the contingency using the HQ staff versus a JTF, the establishing CCDR's J-1 will coordinate with the staff directorates to identify and validate required augmentation to the establishing CCDR's staff. Prior to completion of JMD validation, the establishing CCDR's J-1 should consider feedback received from Service components. Upon CCDR's validation of JMD, the establishing J-1 will forward the JIA tasking message to Service components and subordinate joint commands as required.

Operation Plan Personnel Annex

Services and their components must be aware of the theater personnel visibility requirements prior to the execution phase. A well-developed personnel annex within the GCC's operation plan (OPLAN) is the best method to widely disseminate theater requirements. When the concept of operations has been established, the J-1 provides input to the OPLAN in annex E (Personnel), which outlines the plan for personnel support.

Global Force Management and Global Employment of Forces

Global Force Management (GFM) is the process that aligns force assignment, force apportionment, and force allocation methodologies to support the National Defense Strategy, joint force availability requirements, and joint force assessments. It provides comprehensive insights into the global availability of US military forces/capabilities and provides senior decision makers a process to quickly and accurately assess the impact and risk of proposed changes to the distribution of forces/capabilities in the form of assignment, apportionment, and allocation. The purpose of GFM is to transform these three stovepiped processes into a predictive, streamlined, and integrated process supported by net-centric tools that integrates risk management.

Flow of Forces Into the Theater

Time-phasing of personnel support and personnel services support assets during joint operation planning is a critical planning consideration. J-1 (J-6 [communications system directorate of a joint staff]—for postal) planners with time-phased force and deployment data (TPFDD) or e-JMAPS experience must attend force flow conferences or planning conferences to ensure personnel support and services support requirements are properly reflected in the TPFDD or e-JMAPS database.

Joint Task Force Headquarters Manning

A JTF usually is part of a larger national or international effort to prepare for or react to that situation. In most situations, the JTF establishing authority will be a CCDR. The J-1 plays a role in determining manpower requirements and sourcing personnel for the JTF HQ. The specific organization, staffing, and command relationships will vary based on the mission assigned, the environment within which operations must be conducted, the makeup of existing and potential adversaries or nature of the crisis (e.g., flood, earthquake), and the time available to achieve the end state.

Organization of a Joint Task Force Manpower and Personnel Directorate

The JTF J-1 is principal staff assistant to the CJTF on manpower management, personnel management, personnel readiness, and personnel services. Basically, a typical JTF J-1 consists of three divisions: the joint manpower, personnel readiness, and personnel services.

- **Joint manpower division** provides policy oversight on joint manpower and management of joint forces and US contributions to multinational military organizations. This includes monitoring JMD fills and requirements and coordinating changes to the JTF JMD as conditions change.

- **Personnel readiness division** provides plans, policy, and guidance on joint personnel issues, to include oversight of joint personnel operations. Personnel readiness plans include development of the manpower mobilization requirements for inclusion in plans and orders. Personnel readiness issues normally are addressed in the plans and operations division of a joint force J-1.

- **Personnel services division** accomplishes actions for the internal staff, DOD civilians, and military members of the JTF. It also includes limited administrative requirements related to DOD CAAF.

Personnel Visibility

Personnel visibility is attained by having reliable personnel data from various authoritative data sources for all US Service members, DOD civilian employees, and CAAFs physically present in a GCC's area of responsibility. Establishing personnel visibility is a joint mission with a goal of providing accurate, near-real-time, readily available personnel information DOD wide in a net centric environment.

Sexual Assault Prevention and Response Program

Sexual assault is a criminal act that threatens mission readiness and unit cohesion. Combating sexual assault relies on strong leadership. Per Department of Defense Directive 6495.01, *Sexual Assault Prevention and Response (SAPR) Program,* commanders need to create a climate of confidence wherein victims can come forward and receive care without fear of retribution or retaliation.

CONCLUSION

This publication is the keystone document of the personnel series. It provides doctrine for planning, coordinating, and providing personnel support to joint operations.

CHAPTER I
ORGANIZATION, FUNCTIONS, AND PRINCIPLES OF PERSONNEL SUPPORT

> *"We would not have achieved our position of leadership in the world without the...capability and courage of generations of Americans...particularly our young men and women in uniform who have served tour after tour of duty to defend our nation in harm's way, and their civilian counterparts."*
>
> **National Security Strategy**
> **May 2010**

1. General

a. Personnel services support is a sustainment function executed at the tactical, operational, and strategic levels by the Services under their Title 10, United States Code (USC), authority.

b. Thorough planning and comprehensive personnel management directly impact mission readiness.

c. Integrated personnel support is a vital component of operational effectiveness and, when executed properly, becomes a combat multiplier for the joint force. To accomplish this, Service components must resource personnel requirements in a timely manner. The joint force commander (JFC) and the manpower and personnel directorate of a joint staff (J-1) continually maintain visibility of personnel manning levels to anticipate requirements and provide timely manpower support to planned operations or to direct the planning and execution of branches or sequels that can best accomplish the task, given existing constraints and restraints.

d. Personnel services support relies on secure and nonsecure, continuous, and survivable communications and digital information systems from the JFC's headquarters (HQ) and each Service. These systems provide a common operational picture, asset visibility, and predictive modeling, all of which are needed to facilitate accurate and timely manning decisions.

2. Authorities

a. The nature of US joint operations makes it imperative that JFCs fully understand and exercise their authority to implement personnel programs and coordinate personnel support functions of their Service components.

b. Authorization and guidance for implementation of personnel programs in support of joint operations are set forth in Titles 5, 10, 38, and 39, USC, and in Department of Defense (DOD) and Chairman of the Joint Chiefs of Staff (CJCS) issuances. Through deliberate planning and crisis action planning (CAP) processes, the J-1 assists the JFC in tailoring a package of personnel programs for every joint operation.

Further information on contingency operations can be found in Appendix D, "Declaration of Contingency Operations."

c. Although personnel services support requirements are coordinated and integrated throughout the operation, each Service and combat support agency (CSA) retains its own distinct culture, traditions, and requirements. Services and Service components will retain authority for personnel support to their forces assigned or attached to joint commands, subject to the coordinating guidance of the J-1 issued under the authority of the JFC.

3. Organization of the Joint Force Manpower and Personnel Directorate

The J-1 section of a joint force headquarters (JFHQ) may be organized as outlined in Figure I-1.

a. **Personnel readiness** provides plans, policy, and guidance on joint personnel issues, to include oversight of joint personnel operations. In some cases it might prove useful to establish a joint personnel operations center (JPOC) to provide a linkage between the J1 and other directorates responsible for current and future operations and plans. The JPOC would synchronize efforts across the staff, subordinate commands, other combatant commands (CCMDs), Services, and Joint Staff.

b. **Joint manpower** provides policy oversight on joint manpower and management of joint forces and US contributions to multinational military organizations.

c. **Personnel services** administers internal staff, DOD civilian, and military members of the joint force. It also includes limited administrative requirements related to DOD contractors authorized to accompany the force (CAAF).

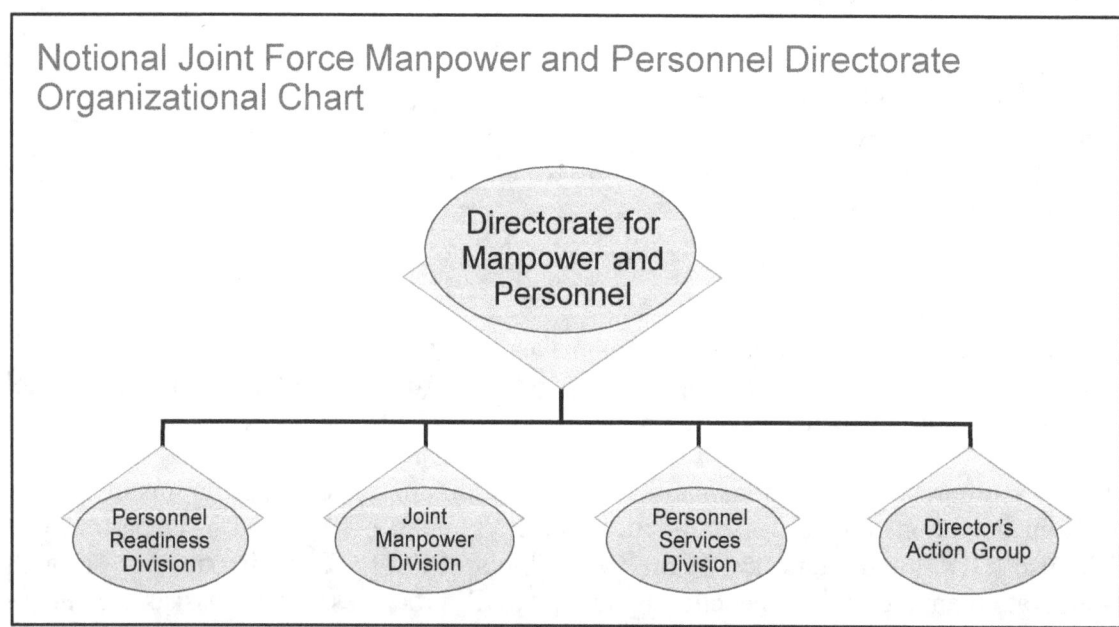

**Figure I-1. Notional Joint Force Manpower and
Personnel Directorate Organizational Chart**

d. **Director's action group,** when established, reviews policies pertaining to the separation/retirement of military personnel, concurrent receipt, survivor benefits, veterans' issues, assignment policy, force realignment and transformation, quality of life issues, compensation, and recruiting and retention.

4. Function of the Joint Force Manpower and Personnel Directorate

a. A joint force J-1's function is to enhance personnel readiness and operational capabilities of the joint force within its operational area.

b. The J-1 is the focal point for joint manpower and personnel actions and, at a minimum:

(1) Participates in all applicable planning and assessment processes and makes specific recommendations to the JFC on force structure, personnel sustainment, and support concepts for each phase of the operation.

(2) Advises staff members on personnel matters that may impact ongoing operations and influence future joint operations planning.

(3) Coordinates with higher, supporting, and subordinate manpower and personnel directorates as well as associate organizations of various United States Government (USG) departments and agencies, host nations (HNs), and multinational forces (MNFs), and when authorized, private and public corporations and businesses.

c. The J-1 may perform other tasks as may be directed by the JFC, but must ensure core personnel competencies are accomplished.

d. To assist the J-1 in the successful performance of its functions, refer to the checklist in Appendix C, "Joint Force Manpower and Personnel Directorate Checklist." This checklist has been developed to assist the J-1 during the planning process and to attain a complete understanding of the combatant commander's (CCDR's) intent and concept of operations (CONOPS). Comprehensive planning by the J-1 will enhance the opportunity for mission success.

5. Principles of Personnel Support Within a Joint Force Command

a. **Command Emphasis.** Personnel support is critical to the success of any operation, and therefore cannot be left to chance or relegated to a minor role. Ensuring the proper planning and execution of personnel support activities is a JFC's responsibility and must receive high priority. The JFC:

(1) Communicates the strategic and operational objectives to the J-1 early in the planning process and refines them as mission requirements change.

(2) Should understand personnel estimates and plans developed to support the operation/campaign.

(3) Identifies and prioritizes personnel requirements to include specific skills (e.g., foreign area language or specialty skills).

Further information may be found in Appendix P, "Language and Regional Expertise Management."

b. **Synchronization of Personnel Support.** Planning and execution of personnel support has a significant impact on other areas (e.g., logistics and maneuver). The J-1 coordinates with other staff directorates and supported and supporting organizations to synchronize personnel support efforts for all possible operational requirements during every phase of the operation.

c. **Unity of Effort.** Timely and effective personnel support is accomplished through detailed J-1 planning and coordination. Integration involves joining all elements of personnel support and personnel service support (tasks, functions, systems, processes, and organizations) with operations ensuring unity of purpose and effort to accomplish the mission.

d. **Flexibility and Responsiveness.** The J-1 must be able to respond to changing situations, unanticipated events, and varying personnel-related requirements on short notice. Personnel support programs, policies, techniques, and procedures should be adaptable to shifting operational situations, needs, and priorities. Responsive, accurate, timely, and relevant information enables JFCs to make rapid decisions. The J-1 needs to identify, accumulate, and maintain sufficient resources, capabilities, and information necessary to provide the right support to the right place at the right time. Additionally, as the mission changes, reassessment must occur to ensure manpower and personnel support remains relevant.

CHAPTER II
ROLES AND RESPONSIBILITIES

> *"You cannot escape the responsibility of tomorrow by evading it today."*
>
> **Abraham Lincoln, 1809–1865**

1. **Responsibilities of Secretary of Defense, Chairman of the Joint Chiefs of Staff, Military Department Secretaries, Service Chiefs, and Department of Defense Agencies**

    a. **Secretary of Defense (SecDef).** SecDef establishes policy, assigns responsibilities, and prescribes procedures for personnel readiness issues as they apply to the Active Component (AC) and Reserve Component (RC), DOD civilians, and US contractors. This includes the Joint Staff, DOD agencies, and Military Departments.

    b. **Chairman of the Joint Chiefs of Staff.** The CJCS, in consultation with the other members of the Joint Chiefs of Staff, advises SecDef on manpower and personnel issues impacting the readiness of the Armed Forces of the United States and the force structure required to support attainment of national security objectives. Additionally, the CJCS is responsible for advising SecDef on the extent to which the major manpower programs and policies of the Armed Forces of the United States conform to strategic plans.

    c. **Secretaries of the Military Departments**

        (1) Functions of the Secretaries of the Military Departments are outlined in the USC and are generally referred to as Title 10, USC, responsibilities. These responsibilities include the functions of recruiting, organizing, supplying, equipping, training, servicing, mobilizing, demobilizing, administering, and maintaining the Services. The Services have a Title 10, USC, responsibility to account for their personnel.

        (2) The Secretary of a Military Department is responsible for the administration and support of forces assigned by him to a CCMD.

        (3) Deployment Health. In accordance with (IAW) Department of Defense Instruction (DODI) 6490.03, *Deployment Health,* the Secretaries of the Military Departments and the Commandant, United States Coast Guard (USCG), (by agreement with the Department of Homeland Security) are responsible to:

            (a) Provide a daily location recording for all deployed personnel assigned, attached, on temporary duty (TDY), or temporary additional duty (TAD) to deployed units.

            (b) Report the data electronically to the Defense Manpower Data Center (DMDC) (at the SECRET level and below) via the Service-specific system at least weekly.

(c) Establish the requirement for each deployed unit to establish, maintain, and report daily accountability (or when changes in location occur) of all DOD personnel assigned, attached, on TDY or TAD to the unit, along with their once-daily location record. Location data is expressed in a six-digit grid coordinate, latitude/longitude coordinates, or a geographic location code.

d. **Services**

(1) To perform the joint personnel visibility mission, Services should provide personnel data to DMDC daily and have the capability to consume feedback from DMDC.

(2) Service deployment systems should use scanning technology to scan, read, extract, and record the barcode data from the following media: a common access card (CAC), a Defense Biometric Identification System (DBIDS) card, a Synchronized Predeployment and Operational Tracker (SPOT) generated letter of authorization (LOA), a US passport, and a US state driver's license.

(3) The US Army, as the executive agent (EA) for the DOD, oversees the rest and recuperation (R&R) program. The movement of DOD personnel participating in the R&R program is captured at the aerial port of debarkation (APOD)/aerial port of embarkation (APOE) in a database. To accomplish this, the EA establishes an interface to provide server-to-server personnel data to DMDC on the Nonsecure Internet Protocol Router Network (NIPRNET) daily. The EA coordinates with DMDC to determine the file layout. Likewise, data for all emergency leave personnel traveling in and out of the deployed theater is captured and reported to DMDC.

(4) The US Air Force is the EA for the DOD Foreign Clearance Program. The movement of DOD personnel in and out of a geographic combatant commander's (GCC's) area of responsibility (AOR) is captured in the Aircraft and Personnel Automated Clearance Program.

e. **DOD Agencies.** DOD agencies formulate and publish policies and procedures outlining the requirement for their deployed, deploying, and redeploying personnel to adhere to the GCC guidance on entry/exit procedures. DOD agencies are also responsible for providing accurate personnel visibility data to the GCC.

2. **Combatant Command Responsibilities**

a. **Combatant Commanders**

(1) CCDRs exercise combatant command (command authority) over assigned forces, which allows them to direct and approve those aspects of personnel support necessary to carry out assigned missions and to standardize personnel policies as they deem necessary.

(2) The CCDR establishes personnel policies to ensure proper and uniform standards of military conduct.

(3) The CCDR utilizes the manpower, workforce, and individual augmentation capabilities in the Electronic Joint Manpower and Personnel System (e-JMAPS) to provide visibility of personnel assigned. Selected data elements will be provided to DMDC on an automated, daily basis by the Joint Staff.

(4) CCMDs require an interface for their unique personnel management and accountability systems in order to establish their daily automated data feed to DMDC on the SECRET Internet Protocol Router Network (SIPRNET).

b. **Geographic Combatant Commanders**

(1) The Unified Command Plan (UCP) tasks GCCs to maintain security and provide force protection for the command, including assigned or attached commands, forces, and assets. From the personnel perspective, this includes force protection responsibilities for all US military, DOD civilians, and DOD-funded contractors physically present in the GCC's AOR (except DOD personnel for whom the chief of the US diplomatic mission has the security responsibility by law or interagency agreement). Establishing personnel visibility and accountability is a joint mission for all organizations in the GCC's AOR.

(2) A GCC has the authority to accomplish personnel service support functions through a single-Service manager during contingency operations. When a single-Service manager is designated, the designated Service component organization will be performing a joint mission, although the organization may not be joint. The single-Service manager will receive policy guidance and direction from and operate under the operational oversight of the GCC's J-1.

(3) The GCC will plan for and cause the establishment of a process, using existing Service deployment and accountability systems, to account for all personnel physically present in their AOR using the Joint Personnel Accountability Reconciliation and Reporting (JPARR) application developed by DMDC. United States Northern Command accounts for Title 10, USC, personnel under the operational control (OPCON) of Commander, United States Northern Command (CDRUSNORTHCOM), and DOD civilian personnel assigned in the continental United States (CONUS). DODI 3020.41, *Contractor Personnel Authorized to Accompany the US Armed Forces,* includes guidance relative to accounting for contractor personnel in support of contingencies in CONUS and worldwide.

(4) The GCC establishes the requirements (standard and expectations) for subordinate joint force, joint task force (JTF), and Service component commanders to establish and operate joint personnel reception centers (JPRCs) within their operational areas.

(5) The GCC establishes the AOR joint mission standards for personnel entry/exit operations at all JPRCs and at each aerial port APOD/APOE/seaport of debarkation (SPOD)/seaport of embarkation (SPOE). Standards, at a minimum, will:

(a) Address establishing a controlled environment, single entry point, check points, and flow patterns for personnel.

(b) Direct barcode scanner capability of all Service's deployment systems.

(c) Establish policy directing Service components deployment systems have the capability to make daily data feeds to DMDC using the SIPRNET.

(6) The GCC should make maximum use of unmanned and minimally manned scanning platforms to passively capture personnel movement.

c. **Functional Combatant Commanders (FCCs).** FCCs will use a Service deployment system to provide data, on a daily basis, to DMDC for their personnel who are physically located in an AOR.

d. **Commander, United States Special Operations Command (CDRUSSOCOM)**

(1) CDRUSSOCOM coordinates on Military Department and Service personnel management policy and plans as they relate to accessions, assignments, compensation, promotions, professional development, readiness, retention, sustainment, and training of all special operations forces (SOF) personnel. CDRUSSOCOM coordination shall not interfere with the Title 10, USC, authorities of the Military Departments or Services.

(2) United States Special Operations Command (USSOCOM) will use one of the Services' deployment systems to provide data, on a daily basis, to DMDC for the SOF personnel who are physically located in an AOR. USSOCOM will interface for their unique personnel system to push data to DMDC on the SIPRNET. If required, USSOCOM will develop the capability to receive automated SOF-specific deployment feedback data from DMDC.

e. **United States Transportation Command (USTRANSCOM).** USTRANSCOM will identify all in-transit visibility systems through the Integrated Data Environment and Global Transportation Network Convergence program capturing movement data on DOD personnel (military, civilian, and CAAF) and coordinate with DMDC to establish electronic data feeds of selected data elements on an automated, daily basis on SIPRNET. USTRANSCOM regulating and command and control evacuation system will interface to push selected manifest-type personnel data elements to DMDC and provide server-to-server electronic handshake data to DMDC on SIPRNET.

3. **Joint Force Command Manpower and Personnel Directorate Responsibilities**

a. **Director for Manpower and Personnel.** The J-1 is the principal staff officer for manpower management, personnel management, and personnel services support. Although the Services have the primary responsibility for providing personnel services support to their Service members, the joint force J-1 will track the efforts of Service components to stay abreast of personnel activities and issues that could impact the joint force. The J-1 develops joint plans, policy, and guidance on manpower and personnel issues; coordinates manpower and personnel support to facilitate the success of operations; maintains a dialogue with other staff directorates, Service components, and outside military and civilian agencies while also keeping subordinate commanders informed of personnel actions that affect their command and their Service members. The J-1 must maintain close coordination with subordinate joint force command J-1s and Service component counterparts, the operations directorate of a joint staff (J-3), and commanders of major deploying, deployed, and redeployment units to provide an avenue to cross-check strength figures and monitor changes to the task organization. Typically, the GCC's J-1, in coordination with the J-3 and the logistics directorate of a joint staff (J-4), will refine or clarify reporting requirements at the beginning of an operation or as it becomes necessary.

b. The J-1 has primary responsibility for the following functions:

(1) **Personnel Management.** A joint force command J-1 participates in strategy development, identifies planning factors, prescribes methods and procedures relating to the management of personnel, and synchronizes subordinate and supporting command personnel to meet the JFC's intent.

(2) **Manpower Management.** Manpower management consists of providing plans, policies, and oversight on joint manpower program (JMP) issues. The JMP is the policy, processes, and systems used in the determination and prioritization within and among joint Service manpower requirements. The JMP reflects an activity's mission, functions, organization, current and projected manpower needs, and, when applicable, its required mobilization augmentation. A recommended JMP also identifies and justifies any changes proposed by the commander or director of a joint activity for the next five fiscal years. Responsibility for the JMP does not fall below unified command level; however, subordinate J-1s coordinate JMP issues. The JMP includes:

(a) The joint table of distribution states peacetime manpower requirements for the current and succeeding five fiscal years in sufficient detail to support Service personnel systems.

(b) The joint table of mobilization and distribution (JTMD) states the additional manpower and organization required to shift to wartime, mobilization, or contingency operations.

(c) Permanent manpower requirements on the joint table of distribution or JTMD cannot be added without validation.

For more information regarding the management of permanent manpower, see Chairman of the Joint Chiefs of Staff Instruction (CJCSI) 1001.01, Joint Staff Manpower and Personnel Program.

(3) **Personnel Augmentation**

(a) Policies and procedures for requesting the assignment of joint individual augmentation (JIA) to meet unfunded, temporary manpower requirements of a CCMD while participating in operations directed or approved by the President of the

United States or SecDef are found in CJCSI 1301.01, *Joint Individual Augmentation Procedures.* The assignment of individual augmentees is usually under TDY (non-unit-related personnel) or TAD (non-unit-related personnel). These policies and procedures are applicable to all CCMDs, Services, and DOD agencies.

(b) In general, the JIA process flows from the CCMD (after the CCMD fills as many requirements as possible from its internal assets: assigned units, staff, Service components, contractors, etc.) to the Joint Staff J-1, to the joint force providers for sourcing determination, and then ordered by SecDef, IAW the Global Force Management (GFM) process. Communication, timeliness, and tracking are essential to the success of this process.

Additional information may be found in CJCSI 1301.01, Joint Individual Augmentation Procedures.

(4) **Joint Personnel Training and Tracking Activities (JPTTAs)**

(a) JPTTAs may be established in a supporting GCC's AOR upon request of the supported GCC. These centers facilitate accountability, training, processing, and onward movement of both military and DOD civilian individual augmentees preparing for overseas movement for assignment to joint or combined staff positions. CAAF should also be processed through the appropriate replacement center per DODI 3020.41, *Contractor Personnel Authorized to Accompany the US Armed Forces,* in conjunction with the JPTTA prior to deploying to the operational area. Policy and procedures governing CAAF, including predeployment requirements and processing at deployment centers and reception centers, are covered in DODI 3020.41, *Contractor Personnel Authorized to Accompany the US Armed Forces.*

(b) JPRCs are established in the operational area per direction of the GCC. Their purpose is to facilitate the reception, accountability, visibility, and processing of military, DOD civilians, CAAF, and individual augmentees upon their arrival in the operational area.

(c) Individual augmentees will be out processed through the JPRC upon departing the operational area and, if appropriate, will be processed back through the replacement center in conjunction with the JPTTA upon return to the US or the foreign location. CAAF are required to process through the JPRC, unless waived by Under Secretary of Defense for Acquisition, Technology, and Logistics (USD[AT&L]) on an individual basis.

(d) JPRCs and JPTTAs should be established as early as possible in an operation, preferably in time to support initial movement of augmentees. All such facilities should be staffed with personnel from each Service comprising the joint force. Additional information on JPTTA and JPRC operations may be found in Appendix G, "Joint Personnel Reception Center and Joint Personnel Training and Tracking Activities."

(5) **Personnel Accountability and Strength Reporting.** Service component commanders are responsible for maintaining accountability of their forces. The joint

force J-1 accomplishes joint strength reporting for the JFC by combining daily Service component strength reports into the joint personnel status and casualty report (JPERSTAT). The JPERSTAT may be incorporated into the JFC daily situation report (SITREP) if the situation dictates. Detailed information on the preparation of the JPERSTAT is outlined in Chairman of the Joint Chiefs of Staff Manual (CJCSM) 3150.13C, *Joint Reporting Structure—Personnel Manual*, Enclosure A—Joint Personnel Status Report (JPERSTAT). The J-1 ensures direct accountability for joint HQ personnel.

(6) **Rotation Policies**

(a) In coordination with J-3, the J-1 makes recommendations on rotation policy for individual augmentees assigned to the JFC. The J-3 makes recommendations on unit rotation policies. Component commanders and CSA directors make recommendations on both individual and unit rotation policies. The GCC in agreement with the Service providing resource establishes individual and unit rotation policies.

(b) Rotation policies are based on a number of factors, including the joint force mission, projected length of the operation, operational environment; requirements for personnel with unique or low-density occupational skills, authority limitations for recalled and/or mobilized personnel, and unit training and qualification requirements. Additional information may be found in Appendix F, "Individual Augmentation Planning and Procedures."

(7) **Civilian Employees.** The joint force J-1 is responsible for coordinating and integrating personnel plans and procedures for civilian support to joint operations. The GCC establishes AOR admission requirements for DOD civilians and CAAF. GCCs coordinate with DOD components to ensure AOR/joint operations area (JOA) admission requirements and other terms and conditions affecting the integration of CAAF into operation plans (OPLANs) and operation orders are incorporated into applicable contracts. The J-1 will identify predeployment requirements to include proper identification cards, security clearances, training, clothing, equipping, and medical processing. For CAAF, the link to the deployment is established by a government contracting officer (or designee)-issued LOA generated through SPOT. The LOA is required for CAAF to process through; to travel to, from, and within the AOR/JOA; and to identify any additional authorizations, privileges, or government support entitled under the contract. The J-1 should coordinate with component personnel officers and the J-4 to ensure that contract LOAs reflect GCC requirements and that LOAs are required at all vetting points processing CAAF. The JFC designates a responsible agent to monitor contract issues (normally the J-4), including administration, and coordinates with the J-1 for any special CAAF issues, including administration support. Additional information may be found in Appendix O, "Civilian Personnel Management."

(8) **Pay and Entitlements.** Based on the unique aspects of each military operation, the GCC will make policy determinations concerning pay and entitlements. The J-1 will make recommendations on these policy decisions. Two key considerations are equity and timeliness.

(a) Equity. Pay and entitlements (e.g., imminent danger pay [IDP] and type of TDY status) should be addressed by the J-1 during the planning process. Consistent policies should be developed to prevent inequities among personnel from the various Services.

(b) Timeliness. Pay and entitlements requests normally take time to enact, so an early policy determination will enhance personnel receiving proper and timely pay. For example, an IDP entitlement is not effective until a request for it is approved by the Principal Deputy Under Secretary of Defense (Personnel and Readiness) (PDUSD[P&R]). It is not retroactive. Thus, personnel will not be considered for any IDP entitlements until a request is approved.

For additional guidance on pay, allowances, and entitlements, consult Joint Publication (JP) 1-06, Financial Management Support in Joint Operations.

(9) Postal Operations

(a) The supported GCC shall assign the appropriate directorate, usually the J-1, to coordinate postal support for any military operation. Those directorate elements concerned with postal support shall be referred to as the joint forces postal staff. The Military Postal Service Agency (MPSA) and the United States Postal Service (USPS) will assist the designated directorate, as requested, in both deliberate planning and CAP.

(b) The GCC may designate a Service component command to act as single-Service manager in providing mail support to a deployed joint force. Planning requires close coordination with the J-3 and J-4 to integrate the movement of mail into the overall lift requirement and airflow.

(c) The designated directorate shall develop postal policies. Below are topics for consideration. Additional information may be found in Appendix J, "Postal Operations."

1. For US-based operations, local postal services should be considered.

2. Postal staffing and equipment requirements and placement of both in the time-phased force and deployment data (TPFDD).

3. Start date for mail service.

4. Establishment of postal infrastructure in the operational area.

5. Postal restrictions and embargo procedures.

6. Free mail.

7. Holiday mail programs.

8. Mail screening.

9. Mail routing instructions.

10. Priority of mail movement.

11. Planning factors for military mail terminals.

12. Contracted postal services.

13. United Nations (UN) operations.

14. Postal support for foreign forces.

15. Postal support to detainee operations.

16. Package size restrictions.

17. Items prohibited by host country.

(10) **Morale, Welfare, and Recreation (MWR)**

(a) MWR programs are essential to readiness. They serve to relieve stress and raise morale. Additionally, MWR programs can enhance force protection when a joint force is operating in a hostile or uncertain environment by providing activities for personnel in a secure area.

(b) MWR programs may include the programs shown in Figure II-1.

(c) The CCMD J-1 is responsible for external MWR support to a subordinate joint force. A GCC may designate one component command to provide external MWR operational and sustainment support to a designated joint force.

Morale, Welfare, and Recreation Programs

- Fitness and recreation programs/facilities
- Exchange and resale services
- Entertainment services
- Food and beverage sales
- Book and video service
- Newspaper issue and sales
- Commercial telephone access
- Internet e-mail access
- Rest and recuperation programs

Figure II-1. Morale, Welfare, and Recreation Programs

(d) The joint force J-1 coordinates MWR programs within its operational area and executes its portion of the external MWR support program. Additional information may be found in Appendix K, "Morale, Welfare, and Recreation."

(11) **Casualty Operations and Casualty Reporting**

(a) Each Service casualty office provides the necessary guidance and information for its Service. Thus, it can successfully manage its own casualty operations and reporting requirements and provide timely and accurate notification to the next of kin (NOK) of its Service members. Casualty operations and reporting and processing procedures of deployed DOD civilians and CAAF who become casualties will be IAW Office of the Secretary of Defense (OSD) and Service policies.

(b) The joint force J-1 casualty reporting requirements are based on GCC guidance and are typically focused on providing timely information to the GCC and the subordinate JFCs to make them aware of status of forces and events under their purview that may have significant operational impact or media interest. The intent is not to duplicate Service reporting procedures. J-1 casualty reporting typically utilizes the Personnel Casualty Report of the Defense Casualty Information Processing System, the operational report (OPREP) 3, event and/or incident report, or the JPERSTAT, depending on the intensity of operations and the level of casualties. Additional information on casualty affairs may be found in Appendix L, "Casualty Operations and Casualty Reporting."

For additional information, see CJCSM 3150.05, Joint Reporting Structure (JRS) Situation Monitoring Manual.

(12) **Awards and Decorations**

(a) The CCMD J-1 develops and promulgates guidance concerning awards and decorations, consistent with executive orders and congressional legislation, as amplified by DOD and Service awards policy.

(b) The CCMD J-1 also facilitates the timely submission of recommendations and supporting information, with appropriate endorsements, for personal, unit, and campaign awards through appropriate channels. Because awarding authority for many decorations is retained by the Military Department Secretaries, preparation and dissemination of detailed plans for submission and processing of award nominations (as early into an operation as practicable) is strongly recommended. Early communication of requests for delegation of approval authority or waiver of policy, questions regarding DOD service regulations, or other concerns are also encouraged. Additional information may be found in Appendix M, "Awards and Decorations."

4. Service Component Responsibilities

a. Service components shall account for all personnel, including AC, RC, DOD civilians, and civilian contractors under their OPCON. Accountability begins immediately upon personnel entering theater, to include short notice operations. Service components will be required to collect personal data, using their Service deployment system's scanning capability, for personnel from other Services and personnel from other organizations who arrive in theater through their APOD/SPOD.

b. In addition to recruiting, organizing, equipping, and training, the Services and their components have responsibility for providing personnel support to their forces. The Services retain administrative control and accountability responsibilities for their forces assigned and attached to CCMDs. USSOCOM organizes, trains and equips its forces, but uses its coordinating authority to interact with the Services concerning personnel management of SOF.

c. A Service component may have the responsibility for operating an APOD/SPOD or APOE/SPOE in an AOR including the responsibility to in-process or out-process personnel; however, various categories of personnel from other Services and organizations may arrive in theater through the APOD/SPOD or depart through the APOE/SPOE that do not require in-out processing. Personnel data capture, through scanning, for all personnel arriving at an APOD/SPOD and for all personnel departing from an APOE/SPOE must be accomplished.

(1) A controlled environment for arriving and departing personnel will be established at the APOD/APOE or SPOD/SPOE and all personnel will process through Service deployment system data collection points using either manned or unmanned scanning platforms operating on the Service's SIPRNET/NIPRNET. In order to achieve initial arrival and departure data, scanning must be accomplished.

(2) A Service component commander may be tasked to collect personal data, using their Service's deployment system scanning capability, for both their Services personnel and for personnel from other Services and personnel from other organizations who arrive in theater through their APOD/SPOD or depart the theater through their APOE/SPOE. The GCC has the authority to accomplish personnel service support functions through the single-Service manager construct. When a single-Service manager is designated, the single-Service manager policy guidance and direction and oversight will be provided by the GCC's J-1. The single-Service manager's Service component organization may be performing a joint mission, although the organization may not be designated as a joint organization.

(3) Service component commanders are responsible for providing accurate personnel visibility and strength reporting data to the GCC for their respective Service.

(4) A planning consideration is to have a minimally manned or unmanned scanning platform installed in each Service dining facility, each Service medical treatment facility, each Service's MWR facility, each Service post office/postal operation, each convoy staging area, and each fixed and rotary wing location providing intertheater and/or intratheater support to capture personnel location/movement data.

5. Other Command and Component Responsibilities

The J-1 provides support and assistance to the office of primary responsibility (OPR) on the following matters:

a. Reserve Component Call-Up

(1) The responsibility for execution of RC call-up rests with the Services. However, while under certain circumstances the initial request for RC call-up authority may come from one or more of the Services, DOD policy stipulates that it is the CCDRs' responsibility to inform the CJCS of the need for RC augmentation and to ensure those requirements have been fully staffed with the Services (DODI 1235.12, *Accessing the Reserve Components*). In practice, the supported CCDR establishes the overall force requirements to conduct a joint operation, but the AC and/or RC mix is established when the supporting CCDRs and the Services source those requirements. This information is then passed to the supported CCDR who consolidates it and informs the CJCS.

(2) Primary responsibility for incorporation of the RC in command's plans and orders should normally reside with the CCMD J-3 or plans directorate of a joint staff (J-5) (in the Joint Staff, the J-4 is the OPR for the 12 interdependent resource areas that are included in military mobilization). The J-1 provides awareness of personnel impact to the force and advises the JFC on RC personnel implications. Additionally, the joint force J-1 should work closely with the responsible directorate to ensure staff augmentation requirements (such as security clearances) are appropriately incorporated in those plans.

Additional information on RC call-up may be found in JP 4-05, Joint Mobilization Planning.

b. Stop-Loss Authority.
Whenever members of the RC are serving on active duty under Title 10, USC, authorities for Presidential Reserve Call-Up (PRC), partial mobilization, or full mobilization, the President may exercise authority to suspend laws relating to promotion, involuntary retirement, or separation of any member of the Armed Forces determined essential (AC or RC) to US national security. While the Services have the worldwide visibility to determine the necessity for stop-loss, the joint force J-1 should work closely with Service components to ensure all considerations that may impact a decision on requesting stop-loss are communicated to the Services.

c. Noncombatant Evacuation Operations (NEOs) and Noncombatant Repatriation

(1) NEOs are conducted to support the evacuation of those noncombatants and nonessential military personnel whose lives are in danger from locations in a host foreign nation to an appropriate safe location and/or the US. Pursuant to Executive Order 12656, *Assignment of Emergency Preparedness Responsibilities,* (as amended), the Department of State (DOS) is responsible for the protection or evacuation of American citizens abroad and for safeguarding their property abroad. This order also directs the SecDef to advise and assist DOS in preparing and implementing plans for the protection, evacuation, and repatriation of US citizens.

(2) During NEOs, the US ambassador rather than a GCC or a subordinate JFC is the senior USG authority for the evacuation and, as such, is ultimately responsible for the successful completion of the NEO and the safety of the evacuees. The responsible GCC may decide to create a JTF to conduct a NEO. The JTF J-1 may have the responsibility for overseeing the employment and operation of the noncombatant evacuation operations tracking system (NTS) in the DOS Evacuation Control Center.

(3) The joint force J-1 is responsible for submitting JPERSTATs for the deployed force. Utilization of the SITREP format is acceptable.

(4) The DOS maintains and updates the F-77 report. The report is an estimation of the number of private American citizens in a country. The report plays a central role in DOS and DOD planning for and conducting NEOs. The report can be viewed on SIPRNET at http://ses.state.sgov.gov/f77/.

(5) The DOD EA for the NEO repatriation process is the Secretary of the Army.

(6) The Commander, US Army Forces Command, and Commander, US Pacific Command, are the EAs responsible for executing the nonemergency repatriation plan on order from Department of the Army Deputy Chief of Staff for Personnel. During a declared national emergency, the Department of Health and Human Services has the national responsibility for the repatriation mission.

For additional information on noncombatant operations, see JP 3-68, Noncombatant Evacuation Operations.

d. **Personnel Recovery (PR) Operations**

(1) The DOD PR system provides a framework to report, locate, support, recover, and reintegrate both military and civilian personnel who have become isolated from friendly forces.

(2) The Joint Personnel Recovery Agency is the OPR for DOD-wide PR matters. This agency provides operational support to CCDRs in planning and implementation of the PR program.

(3) The joint force J-1 role in PR includes accountability and reporting, and to ensure Service activities are timely and coordinated with the CCMD. The J-1 should be the principal staff member to:

(a) Ensure Department of Defense (DD) Form 2812, *Commander's Preliminary Assessment and Recommendation Regarding Missing Person,* has been submitted by the unit to the affected Service, as necessary, under the provisions of DODI 2310.05, *Accounting for Missing Persons—Boards of Inquiry.*

(b) Coordinate the reintegration requirements per DODI 2310.4, *Repatriation of Prisoners of War (POW), Hostages, Peacetime Government Detainees and Other Missing or Isolated Personnel.*

For additional information on PR and repatriation, see JP 3-50, Personnel Recovery.

   e. **Detainee Operations**

      (1) The Secretary of the Army is the designated DOD EA for the administration of the DOD detainee program.

      (2) The CJCS ensures the Joint Staff acts on policy, political, military, and other issues involved in the execution of the DOD Detainee Affairs Program and provides appropriate oversight to the CCDRs to ensure their detainee operations policies and procedures are consistent with Department of Defense Directive (DODD) 2310.01, *The Department of Defense Detainee Program.*

      (3) The Joint Staff J-1 will assist in the sourcing process of any joint manning requirements associated with detainee operations.

      (4) CCDRs are responsible for planning, execution, and oversight of detainee operations IAW DODD 2310.01, *The Department of Defense Detainee Program.*

      (5) Subordinate JFCs and component commanders are primarily responsible for ensuring that detainees are treated humanely at all times; that polices relating to detainee operations are effectively implemented and monitored, and measures are in place to ensure compliance; and that personnel conducting detainee operations understand their respective roles and responsibilities.

      (6) The commander, detainee operations (CDO), is responsible for all detention facility and interrogation operations within the JOA.

      (7) The detention facility commander is the commander and/or chief responsible for the execution of all detention facility operations.

      (8) The National Detainee Reporting Center (NDRC) serves as the national collection center for detainee information and is the central agency responsible for maintaining information on all detainees within the assigned theater. The theater detainee reporting center (TDRC) functions as the field operations agency for the NDRC. The TDRC reports all detainee data directly to the NDRC.

      (9) The joint interrogation and debriefing center commander is the officer responsible to the CDO for all matters relating to interrogation, intelligence collection and reporting, and interaction with other agencies involved in the intelligence and/or evidence gathering process.

      (10) Other individuals with specific responsibilities regarding detainee operations are intelligence analysts, human intelligence (HUMINT) collectors, interpreters and translators, the HUMINT/counterintelligence officer and collection manager, civil affairs (CA) officers, military information support operations officers, medical personnel, staff judge advocate/legal advisors, chaplains, engineers, interagency

representatives, multinational representatives, inspectors general, and JFC public affairs officers.

(11) The joint force J-1 is responsible for coordinating personnel services, postal, and MWR support for US military personnel supporting joint detainee operations.

(12) The GCC is responsible for planning the procedures for establishing mail service to detainees.

For additional guidance on personnel services support for detainees, see JP 3-63, Detainee Operations.

6. Other Operational Considerations

Although not applicable in all situations, the following issues should be considered when planning personnel support to joint operations.

a. **Single-Service Manager.** Although each Service is responsible for the personnel support of its forces, the GCC may determine that centralized servicing of some functions (mail, MWR, capturing personnel visibility data, and other appropriate areas) would be beneficial within the theater or designated operational area. If so determined, the GCC may assign responsibility for providing or coordinating support for all Service components in the designated theater or operational area to a single component.

b. **Uniform Policies.** Policies governing uniform wear for deployed military and civilian personnel is a Service responsibility; however, the GCC may establish basic uniform standards in the AOR. These standards might address issues that impact or are directly related to the mission of the joint force. The CCDR, subordinate JFC, or component commander may require that CAAF be issued and be prepared to wear organizational clothing and individual equipment, to include chemical, biological, and radiological element and high-yield explosive defensive equipment, necessary to ensure CAAF security and safety.

c. **Evaluation Reports.** Performance evaluation reports are a Service responsibility. Each Service has specific policies and directives concerning evaluations. During deployments or other situations where members of several Services work together on a temporary basis, the GCC may wish to set basic guidance concerning performance reports and establish evaluation report periods for deployed personnel that coincide with Service-specific guidance. Computer-based aids such as fitness reports and/or evaluation programs and applicable Service publications need to be available to any JFC responsible for personnel from other Services. The joint force J-1 monitors the timely completion and submission of evaluation reports.

Additional information may be found in Appendix N, "Performance Reporting and Tracking."

d. **Passports and Visas**

(1) Increased emphasis on regional engagement has caused more frequent deployments worldwide. DOD civilian employees traveling outside the US on official travel to a foreign country requiring a US passport will be provided an official US passport, to include visas when required, at no expense. For CAAF personnel, support is generally specified by the terms of their contract, to include provisions for passports and visas.

(2) Passport requirements may generally only be waived for US military personnel. In this case, all deploying military personnel must have valid military identification cards and travel orders in their possession. Additionally, the JFC may require that military personnel stationed in, or reporting to, the theater or AOR maintain a copy of their birth certificate or substantiating document to simplify procurement of a passport should the need arise.

(3) Policies for obtaining no-fee or official passports are set forth in DODD 1000.21, *DOD Passport and Passport Agent Services.*

(4) Contractors are required to comply with HN or destination country laws and regulations regarding visa and passport requirements. US citizens and third-country national contractors entering the JOA will have this information documented in SPOT.

e. **Personnel Accountability in Conjunction With Natural or Man-Made Disasters.**

(1) When a natural/man-made disaster or catastrophic event occurs, the CJCS will provide guidance regarding personnel accountability. When directed, CCDRs and the Services will provide OPREPs in order for the CJCS and SecDef to gain and maintain situational awareness of the operational environment within the disaster area.

(2) Each Service has a Web-based accountability and assessment system for reporting that interfaces with the Personnel Accountability Reporting System (PARS). PARS is the central repository that is used to accomplish personnel accountability reporting upon the occurrence of a natural or man-made disaster.

For more information on the process for accomplishing personnel accountability for a disaster and the use of PARS, see DODI 3001.02, Personnel Accountability in Conjunction With Natural or Manmade Disasters.

Further information may be found in Appendix E, "National Disaster and Catastrophic Event Actions."

f. **Multinational Operations**

(1) Multinational operations describe military actions conducted by forces of two or more nations, typically organized within the structure of an alliance or coalition.

(2) Whether operating within an alliance or a coalition, participation of US forces in these missions dictates a comprehensive approach that includes the interagency community, MNFs, nongovernmental organizations (NGOs), and intergovernmental organizations (IGOs).

(3) US-led JTFs should expect to participate as part of an MNF in most future military endeavors throughout the range of military operations. Such participation with MNFs may be more complex than US unilateral organization, planning, and operations. Complex matters (e.g., information sharing, communications system, intelligence, personnel support and logistic support) may be complicated further when planned and executed in conjunction with MNFs.

For further information on personnel support considerations for multinational operations, see Appendix Q, "Personnel Support to Multinational Operations, *and JP 3-16,* Multinational Operations."

g. **Redeployment Operations**

(1) As military forces prepare for redeployment, the focus of personnel support by the joint force J-1 is three-fold: managing the personnel flow to home station; drawing down, reorganizing, and closing out the personnel services support structure in the JOA; and continuing to provide personnel support to those forces remaining in the JOA.

(2) Service components may be required to collect personal data, using their Service system scanning capability, for personnel from other Services and personnel from other organizations who depart the theater through their APOE/SPOE.

(3) There should be no confusion between the personnel community's core functional responsibilities for personnel accountability and strength reporting and the logistic community's core functional responsibilities for force tracking.

(4) Selected personnel data elements of force tracking data systems must become an established automated feed to DMDC to assist in GCC personnel visibility.

Intentionally Blank

CHAPTER III
JOINT PERSONNEL PLANNING

> *"Nothing succeeds in war except in consequence of a well prepared plan."*
>
> **Napoleon I, 1769–1821**

1. General

a. Joint personnel planning is the means by which the J-1 envisions the desired end state in support of the commander's mission requirements. Planning establishes the methods for understanding the situation and analyzing a mission; developing, analyzing, and comparing courses of action (COAs); selecting the most favorable COA; and producing the personnel annex for the command's plans and orders. Successful planning identifies and communicates the intent, expected requirements, and outcomes to be achieved in joint personnel support operations.

b. Effective planning for personnel support to joint operations can support the ability of the CCDR, JFC, and commander, joint task force (CJTF), to accomplish the mission. The J-1 must be fully involved in all phases of deliberate planning and CAP efforts and collaborate with other staff directors in the preparation of the commander's estimate, plan development, and force flow conferencing. J-1s validate and assess the requirements and sourcing of all staff augmentation on the HQ joint manning document (JMD). The J-1 coordinates the early arrival in theater of personnel support capable organizations that perform postal, casualty, award, and personnel accountability functions.

2. Personnel Estimate

The purpose of the personnel estimate is to collect and analyze relevant information for developing (within the time limits and available information) the most effective solution to a problem. The J-1 assists the commander in reaching a decision by estimating whether a particular operation or mission is supportable from a personnel perspective. The personnel estimate process is applicable to any operational situation and to any level of command. It is used in both the deliberate planning and CAP processes. Information on preparation of the personnel estimate may be found in Appendix A, "Personnel Estimate," and CJCSM 3122.01, *Joint Operation Planning and Execution System (JOPES) Volume I (Planning Policies and Procedures)*.

3. Joint Manning Document Development

a. There are required steps to effectively transition a single-Service organization from its routine Service-related missions to that of a JTF HQ. Key to this process is creating a JMD that will define the JTF HQ's overall manpower requirements needed to complete its mission. The JMD can be filled through multiple sourcing methods to include units, coalition, other government agencies, and contractors. The JMD provides the venue for requesting the JIA necessary to staff the JTF HQ.

b. Once a mission is delineated via SecDef orders, the unit identified to form the core of the JTF HQ must identify its personnel requirements. These requirements are translated into a JMD to ensure adequate manning levels with a proper mix of military and civilian personnel with the correct skills to ensure mission success.

c. Joint Manning Document Creation and Validation

(1) JTF Roles. The CJTF, in concert with the establishing commander's staff, develops and organizes a draft JTF JMD that will be forwarded for the establishing commander's validation and approval.

(a) This document provides the baseline for JTF HQ staffing and is used for strength reporting, personnel accounting, awards eligibility determination, base support, and a host of other services and functions. The staffing requirements associated with the JTF HQ are organized based on specific mission requirements.

(b) During JMD development, the CJTF will evaluate current personnel resources available to meet requirements. The CJTF must seek to fill as many requirements as possible from CJTF's immediate available personnel assets consistent with mission requirements and guidelines for forming a JTF. The CCMD J-1 will attempt to fill any remaining vacancies in JMD billets from internal assets prior to requesting Joint Staff J-1 for JIA support (IAW CJCSI 1301.01, *Joint Individual Augmentation Procedures*).

(c) At a minimum, the JMD must contain the following critical elements: command, activity, department, line number, billet title, duty description, grade, skill/specialty, security clearance, source type, service, location, latest arrival date, and tour length.

(2) Establishing CCDR Roles. If the establishing CCDR decides to direct the contingency using the HQ staff versus a JTF, the establishing CCDR's J-1 will coordinate with the staff directorates to identify and validate required augmentation to the establishing CCDR's staff. Once that is determined, the establishing CCDR should provide this initial draft JMD to the Service components to effect planning for sourcing their respective portions. The JMD is a living document subject to refinement due to changing mission requirements or other factors that increase or decrease personnel requirements. Prior to completion of JMD validation, the establishing CCDR's J-1 should consider feedback received from Service components. The end product of this coordination and CCDR approval will be a validated JMD. The establishing CCDR's J-1 will review the final product. Upon CCDR's validation of JMD, the establishing J-1 will forward the JIA tasking message to Service components and subordinate joint commands as required.

d. The establishing CCDR's J-1 is responsible for maintenance of the JMD. Any subsequent additions, deletions, or changes to the JTF JMD must be coordinated via official correspondence.

e. A formalized, structured JMD working group (WG) should be established at the CCMD, joint force command, and JTF levels to confirm/validate their JMD positions by skill, grade, and component; track by-name arrivals and departures for each position; determine/refine current and future manning requirements; and submit requests to higher HQ to change the JMD based on approved additions, deletions, and modifications identified by the JMD WG. The JMD WG, chaired by J-1 with a co-chair from J-3, meets on a recurring basis with a set agenda with all staff sections participating.

f. Early, frequent, and inclusive engagement with the Services during JMD validation and sourcing results in improved fill rates and fewer reclamas to the JIA tasking message or revisions. As such, whenever practicable, theater Service component manpower representatives should be included in the JMD WG.

4. Operation Plan Personnel Annex

Planning is the key to ensuring accurate personnel visibility data reporting. Services and their components must be aware of the theater personnel visibility requirements prior to the execution phase. A well-developed personnel annex within the GCC's OPLAN is the best method to widely disseminate theater requirements. When the CONOPS has been established, the J-1 provides input to the OPLAN in annex E (Personnel), which outlines the plan for personnel support. The format for preparation of an OPLAN personnel annex is included in CJCSM 3122.03, *Joint Operation Planning and Execution System (JOPES), Volume II (Planning Formats)*. Additional information is included in Appendix B, "Sample Operation Plan Annex E (Personnel). Specifically, this plan must incorporate the provisions and functions outlined in Chapter II, "Roles and Responsibilities," paragraph 3, "Joint Force Command Manpower and Personnel Directorate Responsibilities."

5. Global Force Management and Global Employment of Forces

a. Introduction

(1) GFM is the process that aligns force assignment, force apportionment, and force allocation methodologies to support the National Defense Strategy, joint force availability requirements, and joint force assessments. It provides comprehensive insights into the global availability of US military forces/capabilities and provides senior decision makers a process to quickly and accurately assess the impact and risk of proposed changes to the distribution of forces/capabilities in the form of assignment, apportionment, and allocation. GFM goals are to:

(a) Account for forces and capabilities committed to ongoing operations and constantly changing unit availability.

(b) Identify the most appropriate and responsive forces or capabilities that best meet CCMD requirements.

(c) Identify risks associated with sourcing recommendations.

(d) Improve strategic ability to prevail in multiple overlapping conflicts.

(e) Improve responsiveness to unforeseen contingencies.

(f) Provide predictability for annual force requirements.

(g) Identify forces and capabilities that are unsourced or hard-to-source.

(2) The Global Force Management Implementation Guidance (GFMIG) and the Forces for Unified Commands Memorandum (known as the Forces For), are key GFM documents. Each one is published in alternating years. Together they define and promulgate the Assignment Tables and the Apportionment Tables for the entire force.

b. **The Global Force Management Process: Assignment, Apportionment, and Allocation.** The current relationship among the three force management processes are complex. The purpose of GFM is to transform these three stovepiped processes into a predictive, streamlined, and integrated process supported by net-centric tools that integrates risk management. Authorities that govern the three processes are as follows:

(1) Assignment. Title 10, USC, Sections 161–167, provide statutory authority for assignment of forces. The President, through the UCP, instructs SecDef to document his direction for assigning forces in the "Forces For." Pursuant to Title 10, USC, Section 162, unless otherwise directed by SecDef, the Secretaries of the Military Departments shall **assign** forces under their jurisdiction to unified and specified combatant commands or to the US Element of the North American Aerospace Defense Command to perform missions assigned to those commands. Such assignment defines the command authority and shall be made as directed by SecDef, including direction as to the command to which forces are to be assigned.

(2) Apportionment. Apportionment is the distribution of forces and capabilities as a starting point for planning. Pursuant to Title 10, USC, Section 153, "the Chairman of the Joint Chiefs of Staff shall be responsible for preparing strategic plans, including plans which conform with resource levels projected by SecDef to be available for the period of time for which the plans are to be effective." Pursuant to the Joint Strategic Capabilities Plan, "apportioned forces are types of combat and related support forces provided to CCMDs as a starting point for planning purposes only; forces are apportioned to support the National Defense Strategy and the National Military Strategy, with the intent of allowing senior leaders to consider the competing force demands associated with the possible execution of multiple plans. Apportioned forces are those assumed to be available for contingency planning as of a specified date. The CJCS **apportions** forces to CCMDs based on the Guidance for Employment of the Force and GFMIG.

(3) Allocation. Pursuant to Title 10, USC, Section 162, "[a] force assigned to a combatant command…may be transferred from the command to which it is assigned only by authority of SecDef; and under procedures prescribed by the Secretary and approved by the President." Under this authority, SecDef **allocates** forces between CCDRs. When transferring forces, SecDef will specify the command relationship the gaining commander will exercise and the losing commander will relinquish.

(a) CCDRs are directed by the UCP, strategic guidance, and various orders to plan and execute for operations and missions. CCDRs are assigned forces that are to be used to accomplish those operations and missions; however, in the dynamic world environment, a mission may require adjusting the distribution of assigned forces among the CCDRs and Services through allocation. Each allocation decision involves tasking a CCDR, Service Chief, or DOD agency to provide a force or individual to another CCDR. This involves risk to not only the providing Service and/or CCDR, but also to contingency plans. The allocation process begins with the supported CCDR identifying the forces and capabilities necessary to execute missions.

(b) The GFM allocation process facilitates alignment of operational forces and individuals against known requirements in advance of planning and deployment timelines. The planning and GFM allocation processes are integrated, iterative processes. There are two GFM allocation processes based upon urgency of the request: annual and emergent force requirements.

1. **Annual Force Requirement.** CCDRs request their operational force requirements for all forces needed during an entire fiscal year. The Joint Staff will work with OSD, Military Departments, and CCMDs to forward for SecDef approval fiscal year allocation orders that best meet all CCDR force requests with the available forces. The Joint Staff publishes the Global Force Management Allocation Plan (GFMAP). The GFMAP is a SecDef-approved allocation order that authorizes the transfer and attachment of annual forces to/from specified commanders and Services to supported CCDRs.

2. **Emergent Force Requirement.** An emergent request for forces is a request from a CCDR, North American Aerospace Defense Command, or North Atlantic Treaty Organization (NATO) for units and capabilities that were not anticipated at the time of annual submission and cannot be met by the requesting HQ, its components, or their assigned and allocated forces. Requests for forces submitted after CCDRs' annual force requirements submission due date are submitted as emergent request for forces.

(c) The allocation process serves two functions: to develop base plans for the annual rotational force requirement, and to provide the forces and capabilities required by emergent requirements. The annual cycle focuses on developing CCDRs' rotational requirements for one fiscal year in the future while the current fiscal year of execution focuses on meeting emergent requirements. The Global Force Management Board (GFMB) meets quarterly and provides executive level direction and oversight for the development of the GFMAP.

c. The GFM process provides CCDRs the forces to best support US military objectives outlined in the Guidance for Employment of the Force using apportioned forces for planning, and assigned and allocated forces to accomplish missions while mitigating military risk.

6. Flow of Forces Into the Theater

Time-phasing of personnel support and personnel services support assets during joint operation planning is a critical planning consideration. There may be an early need for such specialists as postal personnel management specialists, deployment system management, personnel service support, linguists, legal, religious, finance, medical personnel, and others. The J-1 (or communications system directorate of a joint staff [J-6]—for postal) must identify these special skill requirements to the GCC during establishment of the theater command and support structure to ensure these personnel support assets are present when needed. J-1 (J-6—for postal) planners with TPFDD or e-JMAPS experience must attend force flow conferences or planning conferences to ensure personnel support and services support requirements are properly reflected in the TPFDD or e-JMAPS database.

7. Joint Task Force Headquarters Manning

a. General

(1) A JTF usually is part of a larger national or international effort to prepare for or react to that situation. In most situations, the JTF establishing authority will be a CCDR.

(2) The mission assigned should require execution of responsibilities involving a joint force on a significant scale and close integration of effort, or should require coordination of local defense of a subordinate area.

(3) Normally, JTFs are established to achieve operational objectives.

(a) JTF HQ basing depends on the JTF mission, operational environment, and available capabilities and support. JTF HQ can be land- or sea-based with transitions between both basing options.

(b) JTFs are usually assigned a JOA.

(4) Execution of responsibilities may involve air, land, maritime, space, information, and special operations in any combination executed unilaterally or in cooperation with friendly nations, MNFs, NGOs, and IGOs, and other agencies.

(5) A JTF is dissolved by the establishing commander when the purpose for which it was created has been achieved or when it is no longer required. The J-1 plays a role in determining manpower requirements and sourcing personnel for the JTF HQ. Guidance on establishment of a JTF is provided in JP 3-33, *Joint Task Force Headquarters*.

b. Composition of a Joint Task Force Headquarters

(1) JTFs may take many forms and sizes as they are employed across the range of military operations. The specific organization, staffing, and command relationships

will vary based on the mission assigned, the environment within which operations must be conducted, the makeup of existing and potential adversaries or nature of the crisis (e.g., flood, earthquake), and the time available to achieve the end state.

(2) There are several options that may be used to form a JTF HQ.

(a) The preferred option is to form a JTF HQ around a CCMD's Service component HQ or the Service component's existing subordinate HQ (such as a numbered fleet, numbered Air Force, Marine expeditionary force, or Army corps) that includes an established command structure.

(b) In some cases, the CCDR may designate the standing JFHQ (core element) as the core HQ element and augment it with additional Service functional experts.

(c) As a third option, a CCDR may initially deploy a CCMD assessment team, or like organization, as the JTF core element. This third option would likely be employed in a location where no military presence currently exists.

(d) No matter which option is employed, the capabilities and composition of the JTF HQ must be a function of careful analysis that has determined the span of control (based on the projected magnitude of the operation) and required expertise (and associated personnel) the JTF HQ must possess.

(3) JTFs may be established on a geographical area or functional basis when the mission has a specific limited objective and does not require overall centralized control of logistics. However, there may be situations where a CJTF may have a logistics-focused mission. In these situations, the JTF will require directive authority for common support capabilities delegated by the CCDR over specific logistic forces, facilities, and supplies. Even as a US unilateral force, a JTF usually will operate in an interconnected joint, interagency, intergovernmental, nongovernmental, and multinational environment in which the CJTF and staff must work with and through many agencies and organizations.

(4) Operational or contingency requirements may be filled through Service components IAW CJCSI 1301.01, *Joint Individual Augmentation Procedures*. However, every effort should be made to fill JTF augmentation requirements from CCMD resources.

8. Organization of a Joint Task Force Manpower and Personnel Directorate

a. The JTF J-1 is principal staff assistant to the CJTF on manpower management, personnel management, personnel readiness, and personnel services.

b. Organization and responsibilities of a JTF J-1 are included in JP 3-33, *Joint Task Force Headquarters*. The actual composition of the J-1 will be dictated by the overall organization of the joint force and the operations to be conducted. Basically, a typical JTF J-1 consists of three divisions: the joint manpower, personnel readiness, and personnel services.

(1) Joint manpower division provides policy oversight on joint manpower and management of joint forces and US contributions to multinational military organizations. This includes monitoring JMD fills and requirements and coordinating changes to the JTF JMD as conditions change.

(2) Personnel readiness division provides plans, policy, and guidance on joint personnel issues, to include oversight of joint personnel operations. Personnel readiness plans include development of the manpower mobilization requirements for inclusion in plans and orders. Personnel readiness issues normally are addressed in the plans and operations division of a joint force J-1.

(3) Personnel services division accomplishes actions for the internal staff, DOD civilians, and military members of the JTF. It also includes limited administrative requirements related to DOD CAAF.

9. Personnel Visibility

a. Personnel visibility is attained by having reliable personnel data from various authoritative data sources for all US Service members, DOD civilian employees, and CAAFs physically present in a GCC's AOR. Establishing personnel visibility is a joint mission with a goal of providing accurate, near-real-time, readily available personnel information DOD wide in a net centric environment.

b. The joint personnel visibility mission does not infringe upon the Service's Title 10, USC, responsibility for personnel accountability, but changes the way the Service's report their joint personnel status on their personnel who are physically located in a GCC's AOR. This data approach leverages existing technology moving the joint personnel community from the present JPERSTAT manual Excel spreadsheet (reporting, consolidating, forwarding) environment into a data validation JPERSTAT environment. This represents a substantial business practice change.

> An analysis of lessons learned and on-site observations of both joint personnel accountability practices and the joint personnel status reporting processes for joint operations reveals shortfalls. Shortfalls include, but are not limited to, seepage at entry and exit locations; current deployment systems do not provide sufficient near-real-time situational awareness of all personnel on the ground; limited scanning capability caused manual data entry creating accuracy issues and segments of the population failing to be captured; latency is impacted by the manual accounting of civilians, contractors, deploying personnel, and redeploying personnel; passengers have the opportunity to bypass the accountability and travel validation processes; and the lack of integration and data sharing capabilities between Service systems causes duplicative Service-level accountability processes at aerial port of debarkation/aerial port of embarkation locations. Planning and preparation must be accomplished to overcome these shortfalls.

c. Defense Manpower Data Center. The DMDC is a major participant in attaining the joint personnel visibility goal.

(1) The Contingency Tracking System (CTS) was developed by DMDC to comply with DODI 6490.03, *Deployment Health*. CTS deployment files are used to identify personnel deployed in support of overseas contingency operations and provide information for medical surveillance programs during and after deployments. The deployments and activations data provides information to determine individual and family member benefits.

(2) The DMDC has implemented the JPARR application consisting of a data repository that consumes and reconciles data from existing Service deployment systems, the CTS, and other authoritative sources (SPOT, Joint Asset Movement Management System [JAMMS], Defense Civilian Personnel Database System, DBIDS, and e-JMAPS). Service deployment systems must have the capability to consume JPARR feedback data in order to give them not only visibility of duplicative and/or erroneous records but visibility of Service members purported to be in a theater who were reported through another Service's system or authoritative source. The JPARR application also provides near-real-time personnel reporting and produces an automated SIPRNET joint personnel strength report and establishes the baseline for congressionally mandated monthly reports. Further, the JPARR application provides the DOD-wide access to personnel data as a net centric service. JPARR data sources are listed in Figure III-1.

d. The supported GCC will establish and publish policies, procedures, and standards to accomplish the personnel visibility mission in their AOR.

(1) Personnel visibility policies will address, at a minimum, policies, procedures, and standards for the collection of personnel data using a Service's deployment system scanning capability and/or JAMMS for the following locations, operations, and activities:

(a) Established APOD and SPOD;

(b) Established APOE and SPOE;

(c) Theater opening operations;

(d) Intermediate staging base, within the supported GCC's AOR;

(e) Deployment, reception, and redeployment operations;

(f) Joint reception, staging, onward movement, and integration (JRSOI) operations (including USTRANSCOM assets);

(g) Reception operations;

(h) JPRC operations;

Joint Personnel Accountability Reconciliation and Reporting Data Sources

Department of Defense (DOD) Deployment System	
Synchronized Predeployment and Operational Tracker (SPOT) for deployed DOD-funded contractors	
Service Deployment Systems	
US Army	Deployed Theater Accountability System (DTAS)
US Marine Corps	Secure Personnel Accountability (SPA)
US Air Force	Deliberate Crisis Action Planning and Execution Segment (DCAPES)
Other databases include, but are not limited to:	
Aircraft and Personnel Automated Clearance System (APACS)	
Defense Civilian Personnel Database System (DCPDS)	
Electronic Joint Manpower and Personnel System (e-JMAPS)	
Defense Biometric Identification System (DBIDS)	
Defense Finance and Accounting System (DFAS)	
Defense Travel System (DTS)	
Integrated Data Environment Global Transportation Network Convergence (IGC)	
Joint Asset Movement Management System (JAMMS)	
United States Strategic Command Personnel Location and Centralized Event System (PLACES)	
United States Transportation Command Regulating and Command and Control Evacuation System (TRAC2ES)	

Figure III-1. Joint Personnel Accountability Reconciliation and Reporting Data Sources

(i) JTF operations;

(j) Buildup, self-deployment, and pre-positioning activities;

(k) Afloat forces on Military Sealift Command or maritime pre-positioning force vessels;

(l) Afloat forces in support of military operations or activities in the AOR;

(m) Supporting combatant command mission or mission support activities in the AOR;

(n) Theater reception activities controlled by Service components and subordinate commands;

(o) Air Mobility Command operations (en route support units and contracted operations);

(p) Passenger movement, port calls, non-unit-related personnel movement, and aeromedical evacuation;

(q) Maritime pre-positioning force operations aerial port operations;

(r) Army pre-positioning stock operations;

(s) Water terminal, land terminal, and air terminal; and

(t) Transient air crews.

(2) In addition, personnel visibility policy will address, at a minimum, policies, procedures, and standards for the collection of personnel data using a Service's deployment system scanning capability or JAMMS for the following locations, operations, and activities:

(a) Theater reception activities controlled by Service components and subordinate commands;

(b) All personnel entering and exiting at all rotary and fixed wing aerial ports;

(c) Intertheater travel (coming from another country outside AOR);

(d) Intratheater travel (travel to countries within the AOR); and

(e) In-country theater travel (travel within a specific country in the AOR).

(3) Scanning will be conducted at all locations and the data will be fed either to the Service's deployment system on the SIPRNET or to JAMMS on the NIPRNET.

10. Sexual Assault Prevention and Response Program

a. Sexual assault is a criminal act that threatens mission readiness and unit cohesion. Combating sexual assault relies on strong leadership. Per DODD 6495.01, *Sexual Assault Prevention and Response (SAPR) Program,* commanders need to create a climate of confidence wherein victims can come forward and receive care without fear of retribution or retaliation.

b. Command procedures should promote a culture of prevention, provide education, training, a response capability, victim support, reporting procedures, and accountability that enhances the safety and well-being of all members.

For additional information, refer to DODD 6495.01, Sexual Assault Prevention and Response (SAPR) Program *and DODI 6495.02,* Sexual Assault Prevention and Response Program Procedures.

Intentionally Blank

APPENDIX A
PERSONNEL ESTIMATE

1. General

a. Staff estimates are the foundation for the commander's decision to select a COA. The staff directorates analyze and refine each COA to determine its supportability. The thoroughness of these staff estimates help determine the success of the military operation.

b. Not every situation needs an extensive and lengthy planning effort. In some cases, a commander can review the assigned task, receive oral briefings, make a quick decision, and direct the writing of an OPLAN in message format. Given an uncomplicated task, this could complete the process. However, most joint operations demand a thorough, well-coordinated plan that necessitates a complex staff estimate process. Although written staff estimates are not mandatory, most will be carefully prepared and coordinated and fully documented IAW JP 5-0, *Joint Operation Planning*.

c. The purpose of the personnel estimate is to collect and analyze relevant information for developing (within the time limits and available information) the most effective solution to a problem. The J-1 assists the commander in reaching a decision by estimating whether a particular operation or mission is supportable from a personnel perspective. The personnel estimate process is applicable to any operational situation and to any level of command. It is used in both the deliberate planning and CAP processes.

d. The personnel estimate should contain a casualty estimate. A casualty estimate is formulated by each Service component IAW individual Service directives to support operations planning, future force planning, and training. Casualty estimates support the following functions: commander's evaluation of COAs, by assessment of force strength for missions within the CONOPS and scheme of maneuver; personnel replacements and flow planning, and allocation among forces; medical support planning, for both force structure and logistics support; transportation planning, including both intertheater and intratheater requirements, to deliver medical force structure and to evacuate and replace personnel; and evacuation policy options to sustain the force by balancing minimal support force footprint, maximum in-theater returns to duty, and stable personnel rotation. Service components in a joint force command will provide casualty estimates to the joint force command J-1, who will then make the information available throughout the HQ and joint force.

2. Responsibilities

The joint force J-1 is responsible for preparing the personnel estimate and recommending a COA during both deliberate planning and CAP, from a personnel perspective.

3. Procedures

a. During the personnel estimate process, the J-1 will:

(1) Review the mission and situation—mission, enemy, terrain and weather, troops, and support available—time available—from a personnel perspective.

(2) Consider force protection and terrorist threat in the operational area and appropriate briefings and actions taken to minimize potential threat to personnel.

(3) Identify the decision criteria that relate to the personnel arena.

(4) Analyze these decision criteria with respect to each COA, identifying advantages and disadvantages from a personnel point of view.

(5) Compare COAs to one another based on advantages and disadvantages of each. Use of a worksheet or matrix is helpful to display advantages and disadvantages and analyze their relative merits.

(6) Conclude whether the mission can be supported and which COA can best be supported.

b. Below is the suggested format established by CJCSM 3122.01, *Joint Operation Planning and Execution System (JOPES), Volume I (Planning Policies and Procedures)*, for preparation of the personnel estimate.

PERSONNEL ESTIMATE

SECURITY CLASSIFICATION

Originating Section, Issuing Headquarters

Place of Issue

Date-Time Group

PERSONNEL ESTIMATE NUMBER _____

REFERENCES: a. ( ) Maps and charts.

b. ( ) Other pertinent documents.

1. Mission. State the mission of the command as a whole, taken from the commander's mission analysis, planning guidance, and other statements.

2. Situation and Considerations

---

a. **Characteristics of the Operational Area.** Summarize data about the area, taken from the intelligence estimate or area study, with specific emphasis on significant factors affecting personnel activities.

b. **Adversary Forces**

(1) **Strength and Dispositions.** Refer to current intelligence estimate.

(2) **Adversary Capabilities.** Discuss adversary capabilities, taken from current intelligence estimate, with specific emphasis on their impact on personnel matters.

c. **Friendly Forces**

(1) **Present Disposition of Major Elements.** Include an estimate of their strengths.

(2) **Own Courses of Action (COAs).** State the proposed COAs under consideration, obtained from operations or plans division.

(3) **Probable Developments.** Review major deployments necessary in initial and subsequent phases of the operation proposed.

(4) **Status of Replacements and/or Augmentees.**

(5) **Civilian Considerations.** Include personnel information on Department of Defense (DOD) civilian employees, host nation personnel, emergency-essential employees, and contractor personnel.

d. **Logistic Situation.** State known logistic problems, if any, that may affect the personnel situation.

e. **Communications Situation.** State the situation, emphasizing known problems that may affect the personnel situation.

f. **Assumptions.** State assumptions about the personnel situation made for this estimate. Because basic assumptions for the operation already have been made and will appear in the planning guidance and in the plan itself, they should not be repeated here. Certain personnel assumptions that have been made in preparing this estimate should be stated here.

g. **Special Features.** List everything not covered elsewhere in the estimate that may influence the personnel situation. For example, identify civil and indigenous labor resources available or essential to support military operations.

h. **Personnel Situation.** State known or anticipated personnel problems that may influence selection of a specific COA.

3. **Personnel Analysis of Own Courses of Action.** Make an orderly examination of factors influencing the proposed COAs to determine the manner and degree of that influence and to isolate the personnel implications that should be weighed by the commander in the commander's estimate of the situation. Include consideration of any foreign languages required and the availability of suitable linguistic support.

a. Analyze each COA from the personnel point of view. The detail in which the analysis is made is determined by considering the level of command, scope of contemplated operations, and urgency of need.

b. The personnel factors described in paragraph 2 establish the elements to be analyzed for each COA under considerations. Examine each COA realistically and include appropriate considerations of climate and weather, terrain, hydrography, enemy capabilities, and other significant factors that may have an impact on the personnel situation as it affects the COAs.

c. Integrated planning for the use of contingency contractors. Identify specific contractor policies and requirements in the operation plan/operation order, including at minimum: restrictions imposed by applicable international and host nation support agreements; contractor-related deployment, theater reception and accountability reporting; operations security plans and restrictions; force protection; personnel recovery; medical support; and redeployment. In conjunction with the operations and logistics directorates of a joint staff, consider how the use of contingency contractors in lieu of military or government civilians affects the nature, extent, potential risks and capabilities, and support requirements (e.g., force protection) in the operational area.

d. Throughout the analysis, keep personnel considerations foremost in mind. The analysis is not intended to produce a decision but to ensure that all applicable personnel factors have been considered to be the basis of paragraphs 4 and 5.

4. **Comparison of Own Courses of Action**

a. List the advantages and disadvantages of each proposed COA—from the point of view of the manpower and personnel directorate of a joint staff (J-1).

b. Use a worksheet similar to the one in the commander's estimate, if necessary.

5. **Conclusions**

a. State whether or not the mission set forth in paragraph 1 can be supported from a personnel standpoint.

b. State which COA under consideration can best be supported from a personnel standpoint.

    c.   Identify the major personnel-related deficiencies that must be brought to the commander's attention. Include recommendations of methods to eliminate or reduce the effects of those deficiencies.

            (Signed) _____

J-1

APPENDIXES: (By letter and title) Use appendixes when information is in graphs or is of such detail and volume that inclusion in the body makes the estimate too cumbersome. Appendixes should be lettered sequentially as they occur through the estimate.

DISTRIBUTION: (According to procedures and policies of the issuing headquarters.)

Intentionally Blank

APPENDIX B
SAMPLE OPERATION PLAN ANNEX E (PERSONNEL)

1. General

The following sets forth administrative instructions and format to govern the development of annex E (Personnel) to OPLANs.

2. Procedures

a. Unless otherwise indicated, IAW CJCSM 3122.03, *Joint Operation Planning and Execution System (JOPES), Volume II (Planning Formats)*, the following format for annex E (Personnel) is mandatory for the Joint Staff, CCMDs, the Services, and the CSAs responsive to the CJCS.

b. Pertinent personnel-related references are listed in CJCSM 3122.01, *Joint Operation Planning and Execution System (JOPES), Volume I (Planning Policies and Procedures)*.

c. Development of annex E (Personnel) will be accomplished in conjunction with, and in support of, operation planning to identify and resolve personnel support problems in advance of plan implementation.

d. Command responsibilities and functional alignments for providing personnel support should be described and defined in sufficient detail to ensure that provisions are made to conduct all essential personnel support tasks.

e. The following format and guidance must be followed in the preparation of the personnel annex.

ANNEX E—PERSONNEL

HEADQUARTERS, USXXXXX COMMAND
City, STATE ZIP CODE
DD MMM YYYY

ANNEX E TO USXXXXCOM OPLAN NNNN-YY
PERSONNEL

References: List documents essential to this annex. See JP 1, JP 1-0, CJCSM 3150.13, CJCSI 1301.01, and other appropriate references, including inter-Service support agreements.

1. Situation

    a. <u>Assumptions</u>. State any assumptions that could influence the feasibility of the personnel annex of the plan. If any assumptions are critical to the success of the plan, indicate alternate courses of action of personnel support.

    b. <u>Planning Factors</u>. Refer to and use approved Service personnel planning factors and formulas for Reserve Component and Active Component forces except when theater experience or local conditions favor otherwise. When deviating from approved methods, identify factors used and reasons for such use.

2. <u>Mission</u>. State clearly and concisely the essential tasks to be accomplished with regard to the purpose of this annex as it relates to the overall mission stated in the basic plan. The mission statement should address the questions who, what, when, where, and why.

3. Execution

    a. <u>Concept of Personnel Support</u>. State the general concept of personnel support to the operation. State operations security planning guidance for personnel matters addressed in the annex. In particular, provide guidance to ensure personnel actions promote essential secrecy for the commander's intentions, military capabilities, and current activities. Also, address arrangements to support the conduct of military deceptions and military information support operations. Address all personnel supporting the operation.

    b. <u>Responsibilities</u>. List responsibilities and cite applicable references and inter-Service support agreements for the following areas:

        (1) Personnel requirements.

        (2) Joint personnel reception and processing.

(3) Personnel accountability and strength reporting.

(4) Rotation/replacement policies.

(5) Noncombatant evacuation operation policies, including requirements for execution of dependent care and reception plans and procedures for accountability of all evacuees. Reference Appendix 11, Annex C, Noncombatant Evacuation Operations.

(6) US citizen civilian personnel.

(7) Non-US citizen labor.

   (a) Estimates of availability and requirements.

   (b) Responsibility for procurement and administration.

   (c) Host-nation contracting and support agreements. Upper level coordination with higher headquarters and other agencies for support of contracting and diplomatic agreements.

(8) Enemy prisoners of war, civilian internees, and other detained persons (Reference Appendix 1 to this annex, if applicable).

(9) Formerly captured, missing, or detained US personnel (Reference Appendix 2 to this annex, if prepared).

(10) Morale, welfare, and recreation.

(11) Casualty reporting.

(12) Decorations and awards.

(13) Pay and allowances.

(14) Travel procedures (to include passport, visa, and theater clearance requirements).

(15) Medical returnees to duty (See Annex Q).

(16) Leave policy (such as special leave accrual).

(17) Combat zone/contingency operation benefits.

(18) Deployability criteria for personnel unique to this operation.

(19) Benefits and entitlements.

(20) Military evaluations.

(21) Civilian personnel policies and procedures.

        (22) Finance and disbursing (See Appendix 3).

        (23) Legal (See Appendix 4).

        (24) Military Postal Services (See Appendix 5).

        (25) Chaplain activities (See Appendix 6).

4. Financial Management. See Appendix 3.

5. Legal. See Appendix 4.

6. Military Postal Services. See Appendix 5.

7. Chaplain Activities. See Appendix 6.

                        t/

                        General/Admiral

                        Commander

Appendices

1 – Detainees, Civilian Internees, and Other Detained Persons

2 – Processing of Formerly Captured, Missing, or Detained US Personnel

3 – Financial Management

4 – Legal

5 – Military Postal Services

6 – Chaplain Activities

7 – Linguist Requirements

8 – Contingency Contracting

9 – Sexual Assault Prevention and Response Program

OFFICIAL
s/
t/
(rank)
Director, J-1

APPENDIX C
JOINT FORCE MANPOWER AND PERSONNEL DIRECTORATE CHECKLIST

The J-1 is the principal staff assistant to the JFC on personnel matters. The following is a checklist of personnel related activities the J-1 should consider in planning and executing operations.

MANAGING THE FORCE

1. Does an information management system, to include robust voice and unclassified and classified connectivity, exist for the JTF J-1 that allows summation of separate Service personnel status reports, including authorized, assigned, and deployed strengths; critical personnel shortages; casualty accounting; and personnel requisitions?

2. Do plans include a current summary of JTF manpower requirements?

    a. Has a position description been prepared for each position?

    b. Are critical positions (critical joint duty assignment billets) identified?

    c. Are minimum grade, security clearances, and occupational skill requirements specified?

    d. Are special experience requirements consistent with pay grade level and military occupational designations?

    e. Are procedures established to identify JTF individual augmentation requirements? Have shortfalls been identified to the appropriate authority?

    f. Are procedures established to identify positions available for civilian fill?

    g. Are procedures in place to evaluate conversion from military missions to DOD civilian or whole-of-government responsibility?

    h. In the event of a NEO, are the positions for personnel comprising the NTS teams shown on the JMD?

3. Are procedures established to capture personnel information for all in-bound JTF personnel immediately upon their arrival?

4. Are systems and/or procedures in place to expedite the timely processing of information when casualties occur?

    a. Is each Service represented by a casualty operations cell?

    b. Are casualty liaison teams formed and posted at each major military medical treatment facility and mortuary affairs collection point?

c. Are coordination and communication channels established between command operational elements and Service casualty cells?

d. Are casualty operations adequately equipped to pass casualty information through channels to department level?

5. Is a rotation policy established and published? Are procedures established to ensure the timely rotation of individual augmentees? Are tour length policies established for military and civilian personnel?

6. Is an adequate personnel strength reporting process established and communicated to Service components and internally to joint HQ staff? Does it include a viable format, able to be compiled by the Services, with an "as of" time established for a single time of accountability (avoid double counting)? Are reasonable deadlines established to allow time for bottom-up compilation and submission?

SUPPORT ISSUES

7. Has a JPRC been established? Are reporting instructions issued, addressing, at a minimum, report date and no-later-than time, reporting location, point of contact (POC) and duty phone, passports and visas, immunizations, uniform and equipment requirements, training requirements, and travel restrictions? If appropriate, billeting arrangements should also be addressed in reporting instructions.

8. Are procedures established by component commanders to accomplish the following Service-specific preparation for movement actions prior to deployment?

a. The opportunity to consult with a legal assistance judge advocate regarding wills, powers of attorney, family law matters, and other legal issues?

b. The opportunity to adjust pay allotments, adjust life insurance, establish direct deposit, and other related actions?

c. Making provisions to pay members while deployed? Is Service supporting pay and personnel activities for both AC and RC personnel identified and included in the planning?

d. Providing passports and visas if required?

e. Accomplishing other personnel actions such as medical screening (e.g., immunizations, human immunodeficiency virus [HIV] screening, deoxyribonucleic acid [DNA] sampling, pregnancy screening), identification cards or tags, Service record updates, including record of emergency data, and Servicemember's Group Life Insurance Election and Certificate (Form SGLV-8286) or electing Federal Employees' Group Life Insurance?

f. Conduct of requisite training, equipment issuance, and other personnel readiness procedures.

9. Consideration must be given as to how personnel will be deployed (TDY, field conditions) to ensure that adequate compensation is provided and prevent unnecessary loss of pay and allowances.

10. Are the following support programs established, if applicable, in the present deployment and/or contingency scenario?

    a. Special leave.

    b. Hostile fire and/or IDP.

    c. Combat zone tax exclusion.

    d. Free mail.

    e. Sole surviving son or daughter.

    f. Absentee voting.

    g. Awards and decorations.

    h. MWR.

11. Are MWR programs, including exchange activities for JTF personnel, planned and coordinated?

12. Is military postal support adequately and equitably addressed in joint force and component commands' plans? Has a plan to provide postal services to detainees been established?

13. Are military equal opportunity (MEO) and/or equal employment opportunity (EEO) support adequately addressed in joint force and component commands' plans? Are MEO and/or EEO counselors forward-deployed?

14. Are procedures in place within civilians' parent organizations to apply the annual premium pay limitation to employees' salaries IAW Title 5, Code of Federal Regulations, Section 550.106?

15. Is a policy in place to ensure DOD civilians are assigned to a unit identification code, are properly trained, and have been issued the proper equipment?

16. Are procedures in place for preparation of time cards for civilians at home station or in JTF HQ?

17. Are policies on differential pay, danger pay, and restoration of annual leave communicated to civilians? Are procedures in place to complete feedback and appraisals?

18. Are procedures developed to process personnel returning to duty from medical channels?

19. Are policies established and systems operational to account for CAAF?

20. Has coordination been accomplished with a Role 4 medical treatment facility to review the well-being plan for medically evacuated Service members?

21. Is SAPR adequately addressed in joint force and component commands' plans?

    a. Have theater-level requirements for prevention and response to incidents of sexual assault that occur during military operations been established?

    b. When a CCDR relies on the installation host, Service, or a component commander to provide investigation, legal, medical, and counseling support, have these relationships been formally established and published?

    c. Are policies in place to promote a culture of sexual assault prevention, response, and accountability that enhance the safety and well-being of all DOD personnel?

    d. Are procedures in place to ensure Service members who deploy to locations outside the US are cognizant of sexual assault issues, as well as DOD- and Service-specific policies addressing sexual assault prevention, prosecution of offenders, and the care of victims?

    e. Are sexual assault reporting procedures in place that ensure DOD personnel are aware of restricted and unrestricted reporting options and services available in the AOR?

    f. Has a 24-hour, 7-day-a-week SAPR capability been established in the AOR?

    g. Are identifiable, trained sexual assault first response personnel, i.e., sexual assault response coordinators (SARCs), victim advocates (VAs), and health care providers, forward-deployed? Is information available to all DOD personnel about the range of assistance options available in the AOR and how to access them?

    h. Is space provided for normal office operations, to include private SARC, VA, and/or health care providers' consultation areas?

    i. Are adequate supplies of sexual assault forensic examination kits, as well as personnel who are appropriately trained on protocols for use and prescribed chain of custody procedures available?

    j. Are policies and procedures in place to ensure that unrestricted reports of sexual assault incidents are referred to a commander with designation authority to take appropriate actions?

    k. Are policies and procedures in place to address SAPR program applicability and services for US civilians and US CAAF?

ADMINISTRATIVE ISSUES

22. Is there adequate J-1 staff to support 24-hour J-1 operations? (Note: The JFC should consider creation of an HQ commandant or similar element to perform administrative functions. If the J-1 is responsible for administrative functions, the J-1 staff must be augmented accordingly.)

23. Are J-1 personnel proficient with the command's software applications?

24. Are procedures established for emergency destruction of classified materials?

25. Consistent with operational requirements, is maximum practical use being made of local labor? Are all policies regarding use of local labor by the joint force coordinated with component staff judge advocate, J-4, CA officers? Note: The J-1 and J-3 should coordinate CA issues.

26. Are J-1 supporting plans developed for the evacuation of noncombatant personnel?

27. Are internal standing operating procedures developed and coordinated to streamline the execution of recurring activities and reports?

28. Are all joint force components provided reporting formats and requirements?

29. Are requirements for Service, joint, and multinational publications identified?

30. Is a Service-specific rating scheme monitoring system in place for the JFHQ personnel?

31. Is draft JFC guidance for officer, enlisted, and DOD civilian fitness reports, evaluations, and/or officer evaluation reports (OERs) published, coordinated with component commanders, and issued to those responsible for evaluation of assigned Service members?

32. Is a POC list developed and published?

33. Has a JMD WG been established?

34. In the event of a NEO, is the required quantity of operational NTS on hand or available from higher HQ or other sources within the theater?

35. Has a procedure to accomplish personnel accountability upon the occurrence of a natural or man-made disaster been established IAW DODI 3001.02, *Personnel Accountability in Conjunction with Natural or Manmade Disasters?* Has a program manager been appointed?

Intentionally Blank

APPENDIX D
DECLARATION OF CONTINGENCY OPERATIONS

1. General

A series of personnel-related laws takes effect upon the declaration of a contingency operation.

2. Responsibilities

The GCC's J-1 is responsible for coordination with the Joint Staff J-1 for formal processing of a request for SecDef declaration of a contingency operation under conditions when a decision for PRC has not been authorized.

3. When Does a Contingency Operation Exist?

A contingency operation is a military operation that is either designated by SecDef as a contingency operation or becomes a contingency operation as a matter of US law (Title 10, USC, Section 101[a][13]). It is a military operation that:

a. Is designated by SecDef as an operation in which members of the Armed Forces are or may become involved in military actions, operations, or hostilities against an enemy of the US or against an opposing force; or

b. Is created by definition of law. Under Title 10, USC, Section 101 (a)(13)(B), a contingency operation exists if a military operation "results in the call or order to, or retention on, active duty of members of the uniformed services under Section 688, 12301(a), 12302, 12304, 12305, or 12406 of this title, chapter 15 of this title, or any other provision of law during a war or during a national emergency declared by the President or Congress."

4. Special Statutory Authorities

Some special statutory authorities automatically triggered by SecDef designation of an operation as a contingency operation are:

a. **Simplified Acquisition Threshold.** For contracts awarded and performed (e.g., local national civilian labor) or local procurements made outside the US in support of contingency operations (e.g., MWR equipment or activities), the simplified acquisition threshold is $1,000,000 (Title 41, USC, Section 428a).

b. **Accumulation of Leave.** Military personnel may not normally retain more than 60 days of accumulated leave at the end of a fiscal year except as authorized in Title 10, USC, Section 701(d), (f), and (g). When authorized by Congress, personnel serving in support of a contingency operation may retain up to 120 days leave until the end of the third fiscal year following the fiscal year during which the qualifying service terminated. Refer to Appendix H, "Military Pay, Allowances, and Entitlements," for details regarding special leave accrual. Special provisions apply to members in a missing status (Title 10, USC, 701[g]).

c. **Payment for Unused Leave.** When applicable, the government may pay for up to 60 days of unused accrued leave (Title 37, USC, Section 501[b][3] and 501[f]). The 60-day limit does not apply to Service members who die from injury or illness incurred while serving on active duty in support of a contingency operation. The 60-day limit also does not apply to members of the RC and retirees who serve on active duty and are deployed in support of contingency operations (Title 37, USC, Section 501[d][1] and [b][5][A,B,C]).

d. **Transitional Medical and Dental Care.** The National Defense Authorization Act of 2005 authorized 180 days of transitional health care benefits to members of the RC ordered to active duty, involuntarily retained on active duty, or voluntarily agreeing to remain on active duty in support of a contingency operation, and served for greater that 30 days. Members and their eligible family members residing near DOD medical facilities may enroll in TRICARE Prime and receive care through the direct care system or use TRICARE benefits to access medical care from authorized civilian providers. TRICARE Prime Remote is not an authorized benefit under transitional health care benefits. Dental care is available for members only in DOD dental facilities on a space-available basis. Members needing dental coverage have the option of purchasing the TRICARE dental program for themselves and family members. Members needing further information may seek assistance by contacting a TRICARE service center or accessing the TRICARE Web site at www.tricare.osd.mil.

e. **Special Pay for Health Care Professionals: Waiver of Certain Board Certification Requirements.** During contingency operations, military medical officers, dental officers and nonphysician health care providers may receive special pay under Title 37, USC, Sections 302, 302a, 302b, 302c, 302e, 302f, 302g, and 303. However, if the contingency operation interrupted the process of completing board certification or recertification, the individual must complete the process within 180 days, which may be extended for such time as SecDef deems appropriate, in order to receive retroactive board-certified pay. The 180-day period begins on the date the individual is released from the duty to which he or she was assigned in support of a contingency operation (Title 37, USC, Section 303b).

f. **Foreign Language Proficiency Pay: Waiver of Certification Requirements.** Military personnel who would qualify for foreign language proficiency pay (except for their lack of certification of proficiency) receive such pay during a contingency operation if the operation interrupted the individual's progress toward certification and the individual completes the certification requirements within the 180-day period beginning on the date which the individual is released from the duty to which the individual was assigned in support of a contingency operation (Title 37, USC, Section 316[d]).

g. **Basic Allowance for Housing (BAH) for Members of the RC Without Dependents.** Members of the RC without dependents called or ordered to active duty for a contingency operation receive a BAH if, because of that call or order to active duty, the reservist is unable to continue to occupy a primary residence owned by the member or by which the member is responsible for rental payments (Title 37, USC, Section 403[g]). Members of the RC on active duty under a call or order to active duty in support of a contingency operation may receive BAH, regardless of the period of active duty specified (Title 37, USC, 403[g]).

h. **Savings Deposits Program.** This program was designed to provide a savings incentive to deploying Service members. For contingency operations expected to last 90 days or longer, SecDef may authorize deploying Service members to deposit, with interest, unallotted current pay and entitlements, up to $10,000.00 (Title 10, USC, Section 1035[f]). Activation of this program may be initiated at the discretion of SecDef, or CCDRs may request SecDef approval by submitting a request through the Joint Staff. Upon approval, deploying Service members may submit individual requests for monthly deposits, in the amount of $5 or more, through their respective financial management offices. The interest rate will be determined by DOD and will not exceed 10 percent per annum.

i. **Expenses Incident to Death of Civilian Employees Accompanying the Force.** SecDef may pay certain expenses for federal civilians who die of injuries incurred in connection with service with an Armed Force in a contingency operation, including transport of the remains and presentation of a US flag to the NOK and to the parent or parents, if they are not the NOK of the employee (Title 10, USC, Section 1482a).

j. **Privately Owned Vehicle (POV) Storage.** Service members deploying to contingency operations for greater than 30 days are authorized storage of one POV, IAW Title 10, USC, Section 2634.

Intentionally Blank

APPENDIX E
NATURAL DISASTER AND CATASTROPHIC EVENT ACTIONS

1. General

When a natural/man-made disaster or catastrophic event occurs, the CJCS will provide guidance regarding personnel accountability. When directed, CCDRs and the Services will provide OPREPs in order for the CJCS and SecDef to gain and maintain situational awareness of the operational environment within the disaster area.

2. Responsibilities

a. The CJCS will monitor the military support provided in response to a natural/man-made disaster or catastrophic event and coordinate with the CCDR on the assignment of operational forces and the standing up of all JTF HQ supporting the effort.

b. The CCDR and the Services will provide the CJCS situational reports through operational channels IAW CJCSM 3150.05, *Joint Reporting Structure (JRS) Situation Monitoring Manual.*

c. The GCC in whose AOR the natural/man-made disaster or catastrophic event occurs is responsible for operational reporting when the event occurs outside the CONUS.

d. CDRUSNORTHCOM is responsible for providing defense support of civil authorities (DSCA) upon the occurrence of a disaster or a catastrophic event in the CONUS and will provide the support, when directed. CDRUSNORTHCOM is responsible for accomplishing joint personnel status reporting for the personnel participating in the operation.

e. The GCC will verify the personnel numbers and locations of all forces assigned to support recovery operations in their AOR.

f. Services will report all forces in the impacted area to include the RC and the National Guard personnel assigned to the operational task force.

g. The CCMD J-1 will formulate the policy to accomplish joint personnel status reporting, using the JPERSTAT, in their AOR and in their JOA.

3. Personnel Accountability in Conjunction With Natural or Man-Made Disasters

a. DODI 3001.02, *Personnel Accountability in Conjunction With Natural or Manmade Disasters,* outlines the tasks the heads of the DOD components must accomplish in preparation for the occurrence of a natural or man-made disaster.

(1) Personnel accountability is a shared responsibility between the commander and/or supervisor and the individual.

(2) All DOD components shall inherently commence internal accountability activities immediately upon the occurrence of a natural or man-made disaster.

(3) All specified DOD-affiliated personnel who work or reside within the affected geographical area of a disaster, as defined by the CJCS, are required to positively and personally check in (i.e., physically, telephonically, or electronically), at the first available opportunity, with the appropriate authority or emergency call-in number established by the DOD component.

(4) PARS will be the central repository used by all DOD components when accomplishing personnel accountability reporting upon the occurrence of a natural or man-made disaster.

(5) Services may implement accountability using their Service-specific personnel accountability and assessment systems when desired to account for their personnel upon the occurrence of a natural or man-made disaster.

b. Heads of DOD components are defined as OSD, Military Departments, Office of the CJCS, CCMDs, Office of the Inspector General of the Department of Defense, DOD agencies, DOD field activities, CSAs, and all other organizational entities within DOD.

c. The head of a DOD component is responsible under DODI 3001.02 to:

(1) Appoint a personnel accountability program manager who will serve as the component subject matter expert on personnel accountability. The program manager will complete and submit a DD Form 2875, System Authorization Access Request, by e-mail to the DMDC, at DMDCPARS@osd.pentagon.mil, to request user account access to PARS.

(2) Provide preplanned guidance and procedures to all assigned or attached personnel so they can establish accountability upon the occurrence of a disaster.

(3) Establish procedures within the component to provide for the most expeditious accountability of DOD-affiliated personnel in the event of a natural or man-made disaster.

(4) Ensure all personnel are provided the necessary information and guidance to check in upon the occurrence of a disaster.

(5) Ensure procedures include multiple and redundant means of communication in case of circumstances in which normal communication means are disrupted or nonexistent.

(6) Ensure that emergency call-in numbers are toll-free to allow maximum opportunity for accountability without cost to personnel.

(7) Provide a telecommunications device for the deaf for hearing-impaired employees.

(8) Provide Military OneSource with 1-800 emergency call-in numbers for posting. Emergency numbers will be kept current for immediate posting in the event of a disaster.

(9) Require all managers, supervisors, and employees over which they have cognizance to understand and accomplish their personnel accountability roles and responsibilities and to understand and emphasize the urgency in effecting these roles and responsibilities in the event of a disaster and carry out annual exercises.

(10) Ensure all reportable casualties are reported according to DODI 1300.18, *Department of Defense (DOD) Personnel Casualty Matters, Polices, and Procedures* and included in personnel accountability reports as required. The DOD components, other than the Military Departments, generally do not have a formalized casualty reporting system. See Enclosure 6 to DODI 1300.18 for the necessary assistance.

(11) Ensure NTSs are in place to fully support the Department of the Army, as the EA for repatriation during NEOs, according to DODD 3025.14, *Protection and Evacuation of US Citizens and Designated Aliens in Danger Areas Abroad* (Short Title: *Noncombatant Evacuation Operations*).

(12) Implement emergency contact procedures as part of theater entry requirements under the provisions of DODD 1400.31, *DOD Civilian Work Force Contingency and Emergency Planning and Execution;* DODI 1400.32, *DOD Civilian Work Force Contingency Emergency Planning Guidelines and Procedures;* DODI 1100.22, *Policy and Procedures for Determining Workforce Mix;* and DODI 3020.41, *Contractor Personnel Authorized to Accompany the US Armed Forces.* All DOD-affiliated personnel, to include civilian employees and CAAF, prior to entry into a possible theater of operations, will have current emergency contact information on file in a centralized electronic database. The DD Form 93 shall be used for this purpose. Emergency contact rosters that may include cellular telephone numbers, personal e-mail addresses, and alternate addresses may be maintained to facilitate communications under emergency situations.

(13) Commence disaster personnel accountability reporting, using PARS, when directed by the CJCS. The only exception is that OSD intelligence community components will complete the manual disaster personnel accountability report as outlined by the Joint Staff J-1.

(14) When reporting is directed, download the baseline population from PARS and report updates to PARS at least daily, if applicable.

(15) Establish internal procedures to monitor compliance with DODI 3001.02, to include monitoring the status of separating Service members with remaining obligated service pursuant to DODI 1304.25, *Fulfilling the Military Service Obligation.*

(16) Direct the component and Service lead exercise planner to coordinate with the DMDC to enable a PARS report capability during an exercise.

4. Personnel Accountability in Conjunction With Natural or Man-Made Disasters Reporting

a. Upon the occurrence of a natural or man-made disaster, the CJCS shall:

(1) Notify the Under Secretary of Defense for Personnel and Readiness (USD[P&R]) each time DOD component reporting is implemented.

(2) Conduct a Joint Staff analysis to determine the magnitude of widespread injury or death to DOD-affiliated personnel, the scope of which is not readily obtainable or is unclear, following a disaster.

(3) Establish, in conjunction with the Federal Emergency Management Agency when applicable, the geographical area of coverage for personnel accounting by the DOD components.

(4) Coordinate with the Director, DMDC, to establish the initial personnel baseline for all required personnel categories.

(5) Identify, and formally notify, those components or agencies requiring a classified reporting capability of the manual reporting requirements.

(6) Coordinate with the DOD components to reconcile the PARS baseline, if applicable, as required until all reportable personnel have been accounted for or until directed to cease reporting.

(7) Establish, in coordination with the DMDC, the specific reporting timelines following the occurrence of a disaster.

(8) Direct commencement of personnel accountability from the DOD components upon the occurrence of a disaster.

(9) Recommend to the USD(P&R) when personnel reporting should be suspended.

(10) Coordinate with the Secretaries of the Military Departments and CCDRs on personnel accounting actions and reports in conjunction with NEOs according to DODD 3025.14, *Protection and Evacuation of US Citizens and Designated Aliens in Danger Areas Abroad.*

(11) Include disaster personnel accountability requirements in national-level and Service-specific exercises when scenario-supported.

b. The Director, DMDC shall:

(1) Provide the initial baseline totals to the DOD components for all specified personnel categories as detailed in DODI 3001.02.

(2) Coordinate with the DOD components to account to the reconciled DMDC baseline as required until all reportable personnel have been accounted for, or upon notification by USD(P&R) memorandum that reporting is suspended.

(3) Serve as the single DOD POC for collecting and maintaining personnel accountability information for the DOD components.

(4) Administer PARS.

(a) Distribute PARS reports via the PARS Web application, and by other means upon request. Ensure all GCCs are on distribution for the daily PARS reports.

(b) Develop, maintain, and update PARS reporting files.

(c) Upon receipt of a completed DD Form 2875, System Authorization Access Request, provide the requester with the data element files for the personnel accountability baseline and reporting requirements. Provide immediate updates as data element changes occur.

(d) Support Service-specific and national-level exercises with the initial baseline data.

(e) Provide a PARS reporting capability in support of Service-specific and national-level exercises.

(5) Assist the assigned Service liaison personnel in enhancing the quality of the Service's data provided to the DMDC Defense Enrollment Eligibility Reporting System (DEERS).

(6) Develop, in coordination with the DOD components, the necessary actions to effect near-real-time reporting for personnel accounting purposes.

c. Personnel Accountability Program Manager. The personnel accountability program manager will complete and submit a DD Form 2875, System Authorization Access Request, to DMDC to request user account access to PARS with the exception of components identified by the CJCS that require classified reporting capability. The Joint Staff directorates, CJCS-controlled activities, CCMDs, NATO US National/Service Support units, and other joint activities will prepare a DD Form 2875, System Authorization Access Request, to request a user account for PARS for their organizations and submit to DMDC.

5. Electronic Joint Manpower Personnel System

a. E-JMAPS supports the Joint Manpower and Personnel Program and is the system of record for manpower and personnel data for the CJCS-controlled activities, the CCMDs, US contributions to NATO organizations, and selected joint activities.

b. The personnel database hierarchy data in e-JMAPS is pushed to the DMDC and upon the occurrence of a natural or man-made disaster, DMDC includes this data when creating a PARS query for DOD-affiliated personnel in a specified geographical area using the data.

6. Service Systems

Each Service has developed a Web-based personnel accountability and assessment system and established Service member reporting procedures upon the occurrence of a natural or man-made disaster.

APPENDIX F
INDIVIDUAL AUGMENTATION PLANNING AND PROCEDURES

1. General

CJCSI 1301.01, *Joint Individual Augmentation Procedures,* delineates the method to request for JIA.

2. Responsibilities

a. **The President or Secretary of Defense.** The President or SecDef assigns missions to a CCDR (designated the supported CCDR) and identifies the supporting CCDRs, Services, and DOD agencies.

b. **Supported CCDR.** The supported CCDR is responsible for determining and validating the requirements necessary to support the mission. Once the requirements are validated, the CCDR is responsible for requesting, through the Joint Staff, and securing the required forces from force providers.

3. Rotation Planning

a. The decision to establish a specific rotation policy depends on the mission, anticipated length of the operation, operational environment, unique training requirements, key positions, and the available inventory of required skills.

b. The nature of any operation necessitates a rotation policy that addresses both mission and individual needs. Morale and job performance will improve when individuals know when they will rotate. This is true for both individuals assigned to the joint force and those who are identified for future rotations.

c. Nonstandard tour lengths may be required based on Service-specific training considerations or operational requirements that adversely affect certain occupational specialties. Planners must consider staffing requirements within functional areas. The mission may require alternating the rotation of key billets to ensure the command maintains full operational capability. Changes in reporting dates require coordination and concurrence between the supported CCMD and the supporting CCMD, Service, or DOD agency.

d. Careful management of personnel rotation is critical to the sustainability of operations. The J-1 must track and coordinate with Service components to ensure timely rotations. To strengthen the support link, message traffic regarding individual augmentation actions should be addressed to all supporting CCMDs, Service and/or Service components HQ (operations and personnel offices), and Joint Staff and DOD agencies. The J-1 must also ensure that individual rotations are properly monitored, so that deploying personnel receive the maximum advance notification possible. Every effort should be made to ensure that individuals receive a minimum of 30 days' notification prior to deployment as a rotational replacement.

e. Except when authorized under the Joint Travel Federal Regulations or SecDef 365-day rotation policy, TDY assignment at any one location will be limited to a period not to exceed 179 days. However, when necessary, the joint force J-1 participates in the decision process to request extension of personnel beyond 179 days, and is responsible for identifying the supporting rationale and justification (to include the list of individuals by Service for coordinating amendments to orders).

(1) Involuntary extensions of JIAs beyond their planned rotation date are subject to the concurrence of the Service or supporting agency. However, the supported CCDR may involuntarily extend JIAs up to 14 days in a combat zone beyond their expected tour completion date. Extensions greater than 14 days, or beyond 365 days, require SecDef approval.

(2) Normally, extension authorization will be obtained prior to the expiration of the 179-day period; however, if circumstances dictate, orders may be issued extending the 179-day period and the request for CCDR or Service authorization submitted after the fact.

(3) A CCDR may elect to approve a blanket extension when units rather than a small number of individuals are required for extension beyond 179 days.

4. Procedures for Obtaining Individual Augmentation

a. The CJTF or supported CCDR will document the requirements to support the mission in the form of a JMD. The supported CCDR will review and validate all JMD positions for accuracy and necessity. SOF JMD requirements should be approved by the theater special operations command prior to CCDR validation. Upon CCDR validation, the CCMD J-1 will forward the applicable JMD billets, along with position descriptions, grade/skill/clearance requirements, specific reporting instructions and desired report date to its Service components to fill. Since the CCDR should attempt to fill all requirements internally, the CCDR should also look to staff, contractors, or multinational forces available, or request support from a CSA prior to asking the Joint Staff for assistance. Billets which cannot be filled internal to the CCDR will then be sent from the CCDR to the Joint Staff J-1, for prioritization and sourcing of any unfilled positions. The supported CCDR should estimate the duration of the position in the remarks of the JMD. Figure F-1 outlines the JIA process.

b. Upon receiving the validated JMD from the supported CCDR, the Joint Staff will start the JMD prioritization and sourcing review process. The Joint Staff J-1 will be responsible for coordinating the process after approving the JMD for sourcing. During the first phase of the process, the JMD is sent to the Joint Force Coordinator (J-31) for sourcing determination on the remaining unfilled billets. The Joint Staff J-31 will work with force providers, which include Services, USSOCOM, OSD/Civilian Expeditionary Workforce, and USTRANSCOM, to fill the remaining requirements. Additional details on JIA sourcing procedures can be found in CJCSI 1301.01, *Joint Individual Augmentation Procedures,* and the GFMIG.

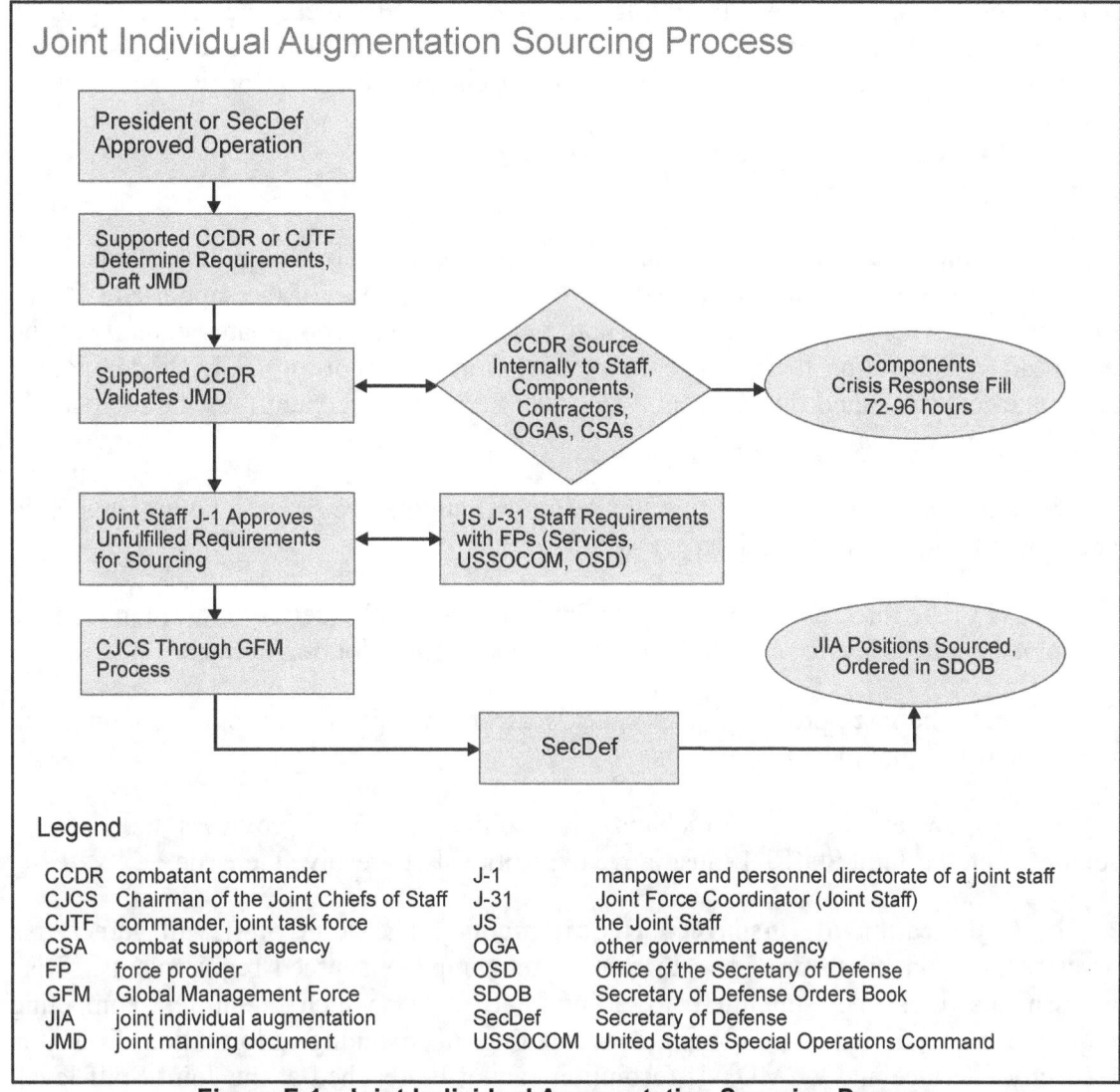

Figure F-1. Joint Individual Augmentation Sourcing Process

c. Force providers will initiate movement of approved IA personnel to meet the requirements contained in the reporting instructions to ensure JIAs arrive at the JTF or CCMD by the requested date.

d. Should a force provider disagree with the supported CCDR ordered requirements, they can reclama IAW the GFMIG and the GFM Resolution Process. The Joint Staff takes the matter for final determination to SecDef.

e. Individual mobilization augmentees are recalled to active duty IAW procedures in JP 4-05, *Joint Mobilization Planning.*

f. The supported CCDR will be responsible for reviewing and revalidating JMD positions at least every 12 months IAW the GFMIG. If JMD positions are still required and validated, they will continue to be filled as previously assigned. IAW the GFMB timeline the annual revalidation and prioritization of JMD requirements may result in the reallocation of specific low-supply/high-demand skills to meet the highest priority requirements. The Joint Staff prioritization process allows for all JMDs to be ranked 1 to X based on the GFM (Force Allocation Decision Model priority) and GFMB concurrence.

5. Key Considerations

a. **Communication.** It is critical that all parties be informed of the status of an augmentation request. This means that the Service components of the supported CCMD, the supported CCMD, the Joint Staff, and force providers coordinate regularly using electronic collaboration tools. When personnel from a supporting CCDR's component are requested, the supporting CCMD J-1 and its Service component must be included in all subsequent official correspondence.

b. **Timeliness.** It is crucial that the individual augmentee process be initiated early and worked as quickly as possible.

(1) The force providers must quickly and thoroughly identify their requirements to provide enough time for JIAs to be identified and prepare for deployment.

(2) The force providers must quickly ascertain capacity to provide commitment to source JIA requirements.

(3) When there is a reclama or inability for force providers to source a requirement, the Joint Staff J-1 must move expeditiously to resolve the issue.

c. **Adjudication of Unsourced Requirements.** The Joint Staff will gather risk assessments from force providers to resolve remaining unsourced requirements. Risk assessments must be submitted to Joint Staff J-31, which identifies competing requirements and details a complete accounting of manning information from the respective Service and CCMD. If resolution cannot be reached at the Joint Staff level, the issue will be elevated, and coordinated IAW the Global Force Management Resolution Process, as outlined in CJCSI 1301.01, *Joint Individual Augmentation Procedures.*

d. **Tracking.** Tracking the flow of JIAs (identifying who is coming and when they will arrive) is the responsibility of the supported combatant command J-1 or JTF J-1. Force providers must ensure that all JIA orders include, as a minimum, accurate information on the individual's grade, security clearance, military occupational specialty/Air Force specialty code/designator, and theater-specific requirement line number. This information ensures that JIAs receive proper organizational clothing, individual equipment training, medical screening, and transportation for their duty assignment.

e. **Service Deployment Sites.** Force providers will man, train, and equip their JIAs to meet the specific requirements of the CCMD validated position. Services require CAAF to use a specific deployment center for deployment and redeployment processing, unless contractor-performed JOA/AOR admission processing (a process that incorporates all the functions of a deployment center) is authorized. Such requirements will be reflected in the contracts of defense contractors employing CAAF. See DODI 3020.41, *Contractor Personnel Authorized to Accompany the US Armed Forces,* for more details.

Intentionally Blank

APPENDIX G
JOINT PERSONNEL RECEPTION CENTER AND
JOINT PERSONNEL TRAINING AND TRACKING ACTIVITIES

1. Joint Personnel Reception Center

a. A geographic combatant command J-1 will formulate the AOR plan for establishing the necessary JPRCs to accomplish the in-processing and out-processing of individual augmentees (military, civilian, and contractor).

(1) JPRCs should be established as early as possible in an operation to support the initial movement of augmentees.

(2) There may be a requirement to conduct JPRC operations at all force entry points. This may require setting up a JPRC "Main" at the primary port of debarkation and satellite JPRC locations at secondary entry points.

b. A JPRC can be established in an AOR, a JOA, or an operational area (per direction of the GCC, a commander of a joint force, or a CJTF).

(1) A JPRC is responsible for the reception, accountability, and processing of military and civilian individual augmentees, including CAAF, upon their arrival in the theater or the operational area.

(2) The JPRC serves as the liaison point for a sponsor to link up with an augmentee.

c. A JPRC is responsibility for the out-processing of military and civilian individual augmentees, including CAAF, upon their departure from the theater or the operational area.

2. Contractor Personnel Processing

a. CAAF are required by DODI 3020.41, *Contractor Personnel Authorized to Accompany the US Armed Forces,* to be processed into and out of the AOR through a JPRC or other personnel center designated by the GCC.

b. Contractors not authorized to accompany the force (non-CAAF) are contingency contractor employees, and all tiers of subcontractor employees who are not authorized through their contract to accompany the force do not have protected status IAW international conventions.

c. The JPRC ensures contractor personnel meet theater-specific entrance requirements and coordinates with the component command or DOD agency to determine proper disposition of those contractor personnel who fail to meet entrance requirements.

d. All CAAF personnel are required to carry a barcoded LOA, issued through SPOT, which allows them access to, travel within, and departure from the AOR outside the US.

e. The LOA will identify USG furnished support, facilities, services, and equipment the contractor is entitled to receive (e.g., billeting, messing, medical, military exchanges, MWR facilities).

f. Day laborers under theater support contracts or hired in theater by external support contractors are not required to process through the JPRC.

3. Reception Operations

In order to prevent any confusion, the "reception operations" concept must be addressed. Reception operations are a series of events enabled by logistics. Reception operations include all those functions required to receive and clear **unit** personnel, equipment, and materiel through a port of debarkation. Reception is the process of unloading personnel, equipment, and materiel from strategic or operational transport, and marshalling the deploying units for movement out of the reception area. Specific items listed within the reception operations include briefings, passenger accountability, transportation to and from JOA, force protection aspects, health issues that may be encountered, etc.

4. Joint Personnel Training and Tracking Activity

a. Upon request of the supported GCC, a JPTTA may be established in the CONUS to facilitate the reception, accountability, processing, training, and onward movement of both military and civilian individual augmentees when large numbers of augmentees and/or replacements are expected to deploy to the theater to support a joint military operation. The JPTTA provides deployment preparation and training to individuals not associated with deploying units.

b. A JPTTA will normally be colocated with an Army replacement center. The replacement centers receive and process individual non-unit-related military, civilians, and CAAF for deployment to and redeployment from the theaters of operations.

c. The supported GCC provides liaison officers to the JPTTA and provides the supporting GCC with the task, conditions, and standards to be taught to deploying personnel. Training is based on the requirements of the supported GCC.

5. Personnel Accountability

During the deployment and redeployment process, there should be no confusion between the Service personnel community's core functional responsibility for personnel accountability and the Service logistic community's responsibility for force tracking. Force tracking is the process of gathering and maintaining information on the location, status, and predicted movement of a unit while in transit to the specified operational area. Personnel accounting is the process of identifying, capturing, and recording the standard name line data of an individual through the use of a database.

APPENDIX H
MILITARY PAY, ALLOWANCES, AND ENTITLEMENTS

1. General

Various pays and entitlements have been established to compensate military members for the rigors and sacrifices associated with military operations dependent on duty status and location. The J-1 has functional responsibility for coordinating pay policy. Proposed changes to pay and entitlement policies must be coordinated with J-4 and the force structure, resource, and assessment directorate of the joint staff to correctly assess impact on these support systems. Therefore, it is essential that the CCDR and J-1 are familiar with current joint pay and entitlements policy and plan for them appropriately. Thorough consideration of pay and entitlements issues in the earliest stages of operational planning ensures they won't later become major distractions for the CCDR.

2. Responsibilities

a. **Joint Staff J-1.** The Joint Staff J-1 is responsible for advising the CJCS; Director, Joint Staff (DJS); and CCMD J-1 staffs on pay and allowance matters. The J-1 represents the CCDR's interests on items forwarded to OSD for action. The J-1 coordinates and collaborates internally, and interfaces with OSD, Services, and DOD agencies on policy questions and determinations. The J-1 works with OSD, the Services, CCMD, CSAs, the Defense Finance and Accounting Service (DFAS) (Expeditionary Support Organization [ESO]), and the Per Diem, Travel, and Transportation Allowances Committee to disseminate pay and allowance information for joint operations.

b. **Combatant Command J-1.** The CCMD J-1 addresses pay, allowances, and entitlements during the planning and early stages of operations and advises the subordinate JFC. The J-1 forwards the CCDR's recommendations to initiate or terminate pay and allowances associated with joint operations to the Joint Staff J-1.

3. Planning Considerations

The CCMD J-1 staff initiates the decision-making process for entitlements affected by the operation as part of the CAP process. The goal is to announce entitlements prior to deployment to ensure consistent pay among the Service components. Planning should address compensation issues applicable to the operation (see Figure H-1). Determination of entitlements should be made available to Service components, supporting CCDRs, and DFAS ESO via official military orders issued during CAP (e.g., warning, alert, or execute order). The following decisions should be addressed as soon as possible:

a. Designation of the operation as a contingency operation (see Appendix D, "Declaration of Contingency Operations") and determination on the Savings Deposit Program.

b. Designation of IDP areas.

Joint Operations Entitlement Matrix

Entitlements	References	Amount	Remarks
Base Pay	Title 37, United States Code (USC), Sections 203, 204, 1009	Current rate	Based on pay grade and years of service.
Basic Allowance for Housing (BAH) and Overseas Housing Allowance (OHA)	Title 37, USC, Sections 403, 405(b), 1009(f) Joint Federal Travel Regulation (JFTR), Chapter 10	Current rate	Reservists can be authorized BAH or OHA for deployments under 140 days if the operation is declared a contingency.
Basic Allowance for Subsistence (BAS)	Title 37, USC, Section 402, 1009(f) Department of Defense Financial Management Regulation (DODFMR) 7A, Chapter 25	Current rate	See references.
Temporary Duty Options and/or Per Diem	JFTR, Volume 1, U4800	Current rate	Combatant commander or commander, joint task force, determination of regular temporary duty, essential unit messing, or field duty. Per diem and incidental expenses payment vary by location.
Hostile Fire and/or Imminent Danger Pay (HF/IDP)	Title 37, USC, Section 310 DODFMR 7A, Chapter 10 Department of Defense Instruction (DODI) 1340.09	Current rate	Specific geographic area must be designated as IDP area. Effective upon approval by the Office of the Secretary of Defense.
Hardship Duty Pay-Location (HDP-L)	Title 37, USC, Section 305 DODFMR 7A, Chapter 17	Current rate (see reference for rates by country/city as applicable)	Specific geographic area must be designated as HDP-L areas by Assistant Secretary of Defense (Force Management Policy).
Savings Deposit Program	Title 10, USC, Section 1035 DODFMR 7A, Chapter 51	Deposit of $10,000 of unallocated pay earning 10% interest	Authorized members serving outside the United States in arduous locations as specified by the Secretary of Defense (SecDef).
Special Storage of Household Goods	JFTR, Paragraph U4770	Permanent change of station weight allowance	For Reserve Component deployment not required to be >90 days.
Cost-of-Living Allowance	JFTR, Chapter 9	Current rate as established by the Per Diem Travel and Transportation Allowance Committee for permanent duty station	Reserve Component called to active duty from overseas location authorized Overseas Cost-of-Living Allowance.

Figure H-1. Joint Operations Entitlement Matrix

Joint Operations Entitlement Matrix (continued)

Entitlements	References	Amount	Remarks
Storage of Privately Owned Vehicle (POV)	Title 10, USC, Section 2634 JFTR, Chapter 5, Part E, Section 2 U5462-U5479	Cost of storage of one POV	Members deploying to contingency operations for >30 days are authorized storage of one POV.
Combat Zone Tax Exclusion	Title 26, USC, Section 112 DODFMR 7A, Chapter 44	Federal tax exclusion of all enlisted and warrant officer basic pay Officer pay exclusion limited to highest enlisted basic pay rate plus HF/IDP pay if received	Areas designated by executive order or congressional legislation.
Career Sea Pay	Title 37, USC, Section 305A DODFMR 7A, Chapter 18	Current rate	Amount based on pay grade and years of sea duty.
Family Separation Pay (FSA)	Title 37, USC, Section 427 DODFMR 7A, Chapter 27	$250/month	Public Law 110-417 (Fiscal Year [FY] 2009 National Defense Authorization Act [NDAA]) authorized full FSA to both members of qualifying married military couples. See Title 37, USC, Section 427d for details.
Special Leave Accrual (SLA)	Title 10, USC, Sections 701–704 DODI 1327.06	Not applicable	Public Law 110-181 (FY 2008 NDAA) made several important changes to SLA.
United Nations (UN) Entitlements and/or Leave	SecDef Memorandum, 27 Jan 1994 SecDef Memorandum, 1 Dec 1994	Not applicable	US personnel may not accept direct compensation from the UN when serving in peacekeeping operations. Special rules apply to use of UN leave.
Career Leave Sell-Back Limit Exemption	DODFMR, Chapter 35	Paid at the same rate as the member's basic pay	Allows members, at their option, to sell accrued leave time in excess of career 60-day maximum or to take leave, or a combination of the two.

Figure H-1. Joint Operations Entitlement Matrix (continued)

c. Declaration of combat zone.

d. Designation of the TDY and/or TAD status.

e. TDY household goods weight allowance reference joint Federal travel regulations (JFTR).

4. Pays and Entitlements Requiring Joint Force Commander Decisions or Actions

a. **Temporary Duty Options.** The JFTR, paragraph U4800, gives the JFC (the GCC is a JFC) responsibility for determining the appropriate type of TDY status of personnel assigned to a joint force performing duty under similar conditions in the same operational area. When practical, it is extremely important that the TDY option be determined and announced prior to the beginning of an operation, as it needs to be reflected in travel orders. Officers and enlisted personnel retain their previous level of basic allowance for subsistence (BAS) but pay for meals. Officer and enlisted personnel do not receive per diem on sea duty. Determinations of TDY status should specifically indicate if and how the determination also applies to federal civilian employees who deploy to the operational area. One of three statuses apply in priority order.

(1) **Regular TDY.** This is the preferred deployment status for operational missions. Personnel are reimbursed for lodging, meals, and incidental expenses at the local area rate. All officer and enlisted personnel retain their previous level of BAS under this option. JFCs should arrange, whenever possible, for government or contracted messing and quarters to be provided to members of the joint force. When meals and lodging are provided, reimbursement for per diem is limited to the incidental expenses and is normally paid after Service members return to their home stations.

(2) **Essential Unit Messing.** Units are directed by the JFC to utilize government meals when it is essential to operational readiness, the conduct of operations, or effective training. This applies only to units and operational detachments or elements, not to individuals. Enlisted personnel retain previous levels of BAS, but pay for meals at the discounted meal rate via mandatory pay account collection. All deploying personnel receive the daily incidental expense allowance. It is effective on the date authorized by the JFC.

(3) **Field Duty.** Designated by the JFC, this should only be used when directed by the JFTR or it is determined the essential unit messing is not appropriate. Personnel are directed to utilize government-provided meals. Officer and enlisted personnel do not lose their BAS, but pay for meals at the discounted rate meal rate via mandatory pay account collection. No additional allowances are provided.

b. **Imminent Danger Pay.** DODI 1340.09, *Hostile Fire Pay and Imminent Danger Pay,* and *Department of Defense Financial Management Regulation (DODFMR),* Volume A, Chapter 10, Special Pay—Duty Subject to Hostile Fire or Imminent Danger.

(1) GCCs submit recommendations for area designations to the Joint Staff J-1. The recommendation must specify the land area (an entire country or part of a country, specific city), sea area (longitude and latitude of points marking the boundary), airspace (usually associated with a land area or sea area), and coastal waters affected as applicable. The area definition should be unclassified. The recommendation should also include a detailed explanation of the threat pertinent to each area (land, sea, air) that justifies designation.

(2) On receipt of the recommendation, the Joint Staff, through the Defense Intelligence Agency, generates a threat assessment and evaluates and coordinates the request with the Services. If approval is supportable, the Joint Staff endorses the GCC's recommendation to the PDUSD(P&R), who has final approval authority. Prior to approving or disapproving the request, OSD coordinates with DOS, the OSD Comptroller, and the OSD General Counsel.

(3) IDP is not effective until approved by the PDUSD(P&R). It cannot be applied retroactively. Therefore, recommendations for area designation should be forwarded to the Joint Staff J-1 as soon as possible during planning. Decisions are published in DOD 7000.14-R, *Department of Defense Financial Management Regulation (DODFMR)*, Volume 7A, *Military Pay Policy and Procedures—Active Duty and Reserve Pay*.

(4) When in an area that is not authorized IDP, a one-time payment of hostile fire pay (HFP) may be authorized. For example, if a soldier is wounded while on patrol (in a country not designated an IDP area), HFP is automatic based on the certification of the commanding officer. HFP is payable at the same monthly rate as IDP.

c. **Hardship Duty Pay—Location.** Established as an additional compensation paid to recognize members assigned in designated hardship duty locations where quality of living conditions are substantially below what most members in the US generally experience. CCMD requests for designation should be sent to the Joint Staff J-1 for staffing with the Service to PDUSD(P&R) who has final approval/disapproval authority.

d. **Combat Zone Tax Exclusion.** A combat zone is established by Presidential executive order. A qualified hazardous duty area (QHDA) is established by Congressional action. Personnel serving in an area designated as a combat zone or QHDA receive certain Federal tax exclusions on military pay. All of an enlisted member's or warrant officer's monthly military pay is excluded from taxable income for any period of a month served in the combat zone. An officer's monthly military pay is excluded up to the highest rate of enlisted pay, plus the amount of HF/IDP the officer is receiving, if applicable.

e. **Entitlements Stemming From Contingency Operations.** Refer to Appendix D, "Declaration of Contingency Operations."

5. Other Pay and Entitlements Affected by Deployments

a. **Career Sea Pay (CSP).** Payable to all members in pay grades E-1 through O-6, except commissioned officers of the Army and Air Force with 3 or less years of cumulative sea duty and enlisted members of the Air Force in pay grades below E-4. Members on sea duty do not lose their entitlement to BAS, but must pay for meals provided at the discounted meal rate via mandatory pay account collection.

b. **Career Sea Pay—Premium.** Payable to members entitled to CSP when they complete 36 consecutive months of sea duty, if otherwise eligible (see DODFMR,

Volume 7A, Chapter 10 for details). Payments begin the first day of the 37th consecutive month.

c. **Family Separation Allowance.** Intended to partially reimburse members involuntarily separated from their dependents for a reasonable amount of the extra expenses resulting from such a separation. Payment begins after a member is separated from dependents continuously for more than 30 days.

d. **Special Leave Accrual (SLA).** Pursuant to Title 10, USC, Section 701(f)(1), certain Service members who would otherwise lose accumulated leave in excess of 60 days at the end of a fiscal year (75 days from 1 October 2008 until 30 September 2013), may retain an accumulated total of up to 120 days of leave. To be eligible to accumulate up to 120 days, Service members must serve on active duty for a continuous period of at least 120 days in an area in which the member is entitled to special pay under Title 37, USC, Section 310(a) (Imminent Danger Pay), or while assigned to a deployable ship or mobile unit or to other designated duty comparable to that specified under Title 37, USC, Section 310(a).

(1) Leave may be carried over from two to four fiscal years in which the qualifying continuous period of services terminates, depending on the circumstances. See DODI 1327.06, *Leave and Liberty Policy and Procedures,* for details.

(2) In addition, pursuant to Title 10, USC, Section 701(f)(2), certain other Service members who serve on active duty in an assignment in support of a contingency operation shall be permitted to retain any accumulated leave in excess of the number of days of leave authorized to be accumulated under subsections Title 10, USC, Section 701(b) or (d) until the end of the second fiscal year after the fiscal year in which said service on active duty is terminated.

(3) Personnel assigned to unit, HQ, and supporting staffs who are prohibited from taking leave because of their involvement in supporting a qualifying operational mission may also qualify for SLA. One-time SLA sell-back, to be sold at anytime, is authorized for enlisted Service members for leave accumulated in excess of 120 days. Under this provision, an enlisted Service member may sell-back up to 30 days of SLA only once (this does not apply to officers). Such a sell back counts toward the active duty Service member's cap of 60 days over a career.

e. **United Nations Entitlements and Leave.** It is DOD policy that normally, US personnel in units detailed to the UN will not contract with nor receive direct payment from the UN; exceptions must be approved by SecDef. US personnel detailed or assigned to the UN for peace operations may use UN leave. When taking time off in the geographic area of the UN force commander's or chief military observer's authority, the personnel may take UN pass or leave as approved by the appropriate UN official, and US leave will not be charged. When US personnel desire to take leave outside the geographic area of the UN force commander's or chief military observer's authority, the individual must take US leave or pass approved by the US chain of command in conjunction with an approved UN leave or pass.

6. In-Theater Limitations on Local Payments

Joint force J-1 and financial management authorities should coordinate limitations on local payments and check cashing to ensure equitable treatment of all deployed Service members. US command authorities, HNs, UN authorities, or other authority may impose limitations on the amounts of cash payments deployed personnel may receive, and on the amounts of currency they may carry when leaving an operational area. A determination also needs to be made of the type of currency, US or foreign, to be paid to US forces.

Intentionally Blank

APPENDIX J
POSTAL OPERATIONS

1. General

a. Postal operations and services have a significant effect on unit morale. Similarly, large volumes of personal correspondence, parcels, and official mail can have a significant impact on logistic operations. Mail is common to all Services and must be processed, transported, and delivered as a joint operation.

b. JFCs have high expectations for timely mail delivery, unrestricted mail services, and free mail in an overseas environment. Although assigned as a personnel support planning function, postal planning must encompass significant logistic functions. Planning for such diverse logistic issues as dedicated air transportation, contracted ground transportation, early deployment of postal forces, robust palletization crews, container moving and lifting equipment, specialized postal equipment, and sufficient in-theater postal facilities are critical to provide support to a JFC. Close coordination and communication with logistic and personnel planners is necessary for successful postal operations planning and mission accomplishment.

2. Responsibilities

The following is an overview of the postal responsibilities within DOD. The Military Postal Service (MPS) provides postal services to the active duty and civilian components of the Armed Forces deployed or stationed overseas (Title 39, USC). The MPS is regulated by both public law and DODDs. Therefore, requests to expand services beyond those limits cannot be made arbitrarily. Questions, concerns, or conflicts should be directed to:

Executive Director
Headquarters, Military Postal Service Agency
2461 Eisenhower Avenue
Alexandria, Virginia 22331-0006
COMM 703-325-9220/9221; DSN 221-9220/9221
FAX (703) 325-9534

Message address:

EXEC DIR MIL POSTAL SVC AGCY, ALEXANDRIA VA//PP//

a. **Department of Defense.** The USD(AT&L), provides policy guidance and direction concerning the use of MPS by DOD components, other government agencies, and NGOs through the Deputy Under Secretary of Defense (Logistics and Materiel Readiness). The Secretary of the Army is the DOD EA for MPS.

b. **The Secretary of the Army**, as the EA for MPS, shall:

(1) Monitor and oversee the MPS throughout DOD IAW guidance provided by the USD(AT&L).

(2) Provide legal services on MPS-related issues before the USPS, the Postal Rate Commission, the Department of Transportation, and other federal regulatory organizations.

(3) Maintain and operate the Inter-Service Postal Training Activity, for the training of the Services' postal personnel.

(4) Maintain and fund the MPSA in the National Capital Region, including subordinate joint military postal activities (JMPAs) colocated at USPS activities in the US. The MPSA shall manage the MPS worldwide IAW DOD policies, and shall not be assigned non-MPS functions, such as internal mail distribution, electronic mail communications, or USPS services in the US.

(5) Designate a general officer (or equivalent civilian grade) to be the Executive Director, MPSA.

(a) The Executive Director, MPSA, shall operate under the authority, direction, and control of the DOD EA for MPS to achieve the effective and efficient oversight of the MPS throughout DOD, the integration of postal transportation and distribution procedures worldwide, the implementation of uniform worldwide postal practices and procedures, and the management and operation of the MPSA.

(b) The Executive Director, MPSA, shall maintain direct working relationships with USPS, USG departments and agencies on MPS matters, and the DOD components to provide management, coordination, and technical assistance on postal matters.

c. **MPSA distributes MPS policy and provides guidance to enhance the efficient and effective management of the MPS.** MPSA and/or JMPA responsibilities are as follows:

(1) Coordinate with the Federal Aviation Administration and Department of Homeland Security on any restrictions that may be imposed requiring the screening of mail.

(2) Coordinate with the USPS to obtain optimum postal support for the GCC. Ensure adequate time for the MPSA, Services, and affected AOR GCC postal staff or service postal manager (SPM) (if designated), to participate in the formulation, coordination, and approval of any mail transportation and/or support contract requirements prior to bid solicitations. The GCC postal staff or SPM (if designated) with the affected GCC's legal and contracting officers will make recommendation changes to all contracts, when necessary, and GCC postal staff, MPSA, and USPS must agree to the final decision prior to solicitation efforts. Any contract modifications and adjustments must be coordinated with and approved by the primary customer's Service representative, the GCC's postal staff, or SPM (if designated), prior to execution. USPS will designate

the appropriate theater-designated contracting officer representative to ensure proper contract execution and expenditure of DOD mail transportation funds regardless of whether the contract is generated by USPS or DOD. GCC will determine the appropriate administrative official and ensure proper technical oversight, contract compliance, and execution.

(3) Advise USPS to implement mail embargo or restrictions when requested by the GCC or DOD.

(4) Upon request from the GCC, initiate action to obtain or terminate free mail privileges and, if approved, promulgate implementing instructions.

(5) Coordinate air and/or surface movement of military mail with USPS from the US gateway to the APOEs and/or SPOEs. MPSA will establish postal gateway teams to accomplish this function. The GCC's postal staff or SPM (if designated) for military postal service will determine commercial and military APODs and the required level of frequency and pouching, sacking, and labeling requirements.

(6) Request personnel augmentation, as required to support operation of APOEs and/or SPOEs.

(7) Establish mail routing, massing, labeling, and distribution information to/from CONUS to the GCC designated gateway. GCC will establish intra-inter theater mail routing, massing, labeling, and distribution information for theater military post offices (MPOs) to be provided to USPS.

(8) MPSA will adjudicate requests for exception to policy received from the GCC postal staff.

(9) Coordinate with the GCC's postal staff, or SPM (if designated), as necessary to ensure continued proper postal service support.

d. **Geographic Combatant Commands.** The GCC controls theater postal personnel and resources, and will establish the priority of mail movement from APODs/SPODs and onward to the operational areas. This management includes authorizing the theater's designated postal transportation manager to select and use commercial and military means for mail movement within the AOR. Employing any commercial air transportation (foreign or domestic), to and from the primary hubs (CONUS gateways and AOR APOEs) not currently authorized or contracted by USPS must be approved by USPS HQ Contracting Office through MPSA (IAW DOD 4525.6-M, *Department of Defense Postal Manual*). The GCC's theater postal transportation manager or SPM (if designated) will select mail transportation routes within the guidelines of USPS and DOD mail transportation statutes to include approving proposed intra-inter theater mail movement contracts (air or ground). The final decision regarding the level of mail service to, from, and within the theater rests with the GCC via the GCC postal staff or SPM (if designated). Any requirements or issues with the level of service to and from the primary hubs in the GCC's AOR must be elevated to USPS HQ through

MPSA. The GCC's postal staff retains functional responsibility for theater postal operations.

e. **GCC's Postal Staff.** The GCC's postal staff will implement all postal operations in the operational area, IAW CCMD guidance. The GCC's postal staff performs the following tasks.

(1) Establish joint theater specific postal policy, procedures, contingency and exercise plans, command regulations, fragmentary orders, and defense message system policy messages; to include funding, for joint MPS theater hub facilities when activity support is not organic to the base or unit operating infrastructure (e.g., mail control activities [MCAs] or aerial mail terminals [AMTs] at international airports).

(2) Coordinate the designation of an SPM, if necessary, to implement postal policies throughout the operational area under the authority of the GCC's postal staff. While primary responsibility for postal operations still resides with the GCC's postal staff, functional management of the theater MPS may be delegated to the Service component commands acting as the support staff of the GCCs to maintain the postal activity with a capability best suited to coordinate joint postal matters.

(3) Coordinate for the establishment of a joint postal cell (JPC) for significant joint operations. Personnel augmentation for the JPC staff should consist of an SPM core staff (if designated), the GCC's postal staff, and representatives of each Service component command. The JPC, when activated, will operate under the guidance of, and assume responsibilities and authority from the GCC's postal staff. If activated, the JPC will coordinate postal operations in the joint force operational area under the authority of the GCC's J-1 or directorate responsible for postal operations. When inactivated, the GCC's postal staff will assume the roles and responsibilities of the JPC:

(a) Coordinate MPS operations at all military postal activities MPOs, MCAs, AMTs, joint military mail terminals (JMMTs), fleet mail centers, and surface mail terminals in the operational area.

(b) Recommend, on request, additional postal restrictions or embargo procedures for GCC postal staff to establish. This may be necessary if excessive mail volume is hampering the flow of mission-essential supplies and equipment into the operational area.

(c) Specify any restrictions for retrograde mail, to include size and weight limitations and security screening.

(d) Request free mail privileges IAW Title 39, USC, Section 3401 (a), this publication, and DOD 4525.6-M, *Department of Defense Postal Manual,* if not previously requested.

(e) Identify, confirm, and maintain the operational area APOEs/SPOEs and APODs/SPODs.

(f) Ensure that individual Service components postal managers develop and maintain casualty mail procedures and directory services.

(g) Provide MPS postal net alerts (PNAs), SITREPs, and transit time information.

(h) Act as POC for all operational area MPS-related queries, congressional inquiries, and service complaints.

(i) Publish uniform procedures applicable to all service MPS activities in the operational area.

(j) Prepare for expedited voted ballot support and holiday mail surge execution to minimize impact to customer.

(4) The GCC, based on a recommendation from its postal staff, may designate an individual Service component command with the responsibilities to accomplish mail movement functions within the operational area. This designation will be selected based on their capabilities. More than one designee may be appointed for operational areas with distinct geographical areas or sectors, or for distinct operational responsibilities, such as surface, maritime, or air. Responsibilities for designees are outlined in DOD 4525.6-M, *Department of Defense Postal Manual,* or its replacement.

f. **SPM.** If designated, the SPM will implement and coordinate postal operations throughout the AOR under the authority of and serve as the liaison between the operational area and the GCC's postal staff. The SPM, with approval of the responsible CCMD directorate, has the authority to adjust planning factors and execution to allow management authority and responsibility of all theater postal resources until affected theater sustainment or stability is realized in the theater, to enable Service component commands and installation commanders to resume limited or full control of their postal resources. This action allows proper integration and distribution of limited resources whenever mail volume exceeds processing capacity. SPM responsibilities are as follows (when inactivated, the GCC's postal staff will assume the roles and responsibilities):

(1) Coordinate joint MPS procedures in the operational area and designate specific roles to the Service component commands.

(2) Identify postal augmentation requirements and coordinate logistic sourcing as early as possible during the planning phase.

(3) Ensure that postal personnel, postal assets, and postal infrastructure requirements are integrated into the TPFDD list in time to support the early flow of mail into the operating area. Planners should ensure inclusion of postal planning when conducting plan development and TPFDD refinement to ensure integration of postal issues to include identifying any potential transportation, personnel, facilities, and equipment shortfalls. Postal issues should be addressed during scheduled planning conferences to include the TPFDD refinement, logistics, and transportation conferences.

(4) Coordinate with the GCC postal staff to establish the start of mail service. Mail service should be initiated as soon as possible after necessary postal personnel and assets have arrived in the operating area. Although the commander may determine that other forces have priority of transportation, this is normally not later than C+30, or 30 days after forces begin JRSOI operations.

(a) When considering activation of contingency ZIP Codes/Army post office (APO)/fleet post office (FPO) addresses, commanders must allow for operational and procedural time constraints when initiating request for mail service. Operationally, JRSOI of postal equipment and personnel can take several weeks to complete. During JRSOI, units are in various stages of movement and it would not be possible to request mail delivery while units/personnel are in transition. Once a post office is established, the procedures involved in establishing ZIP Codes can begin and are as follows:

1. The SPM requests ZIP Code establishment.

2. MPSA assigns a five-digit number based on available ZIP Codes for a geographical region.

3. MPSA notifies JMPA and USPS HQ.

4. JMPA puts ZIP Code information into the Address Management System and Global Enterprise Mail System and assigns mail routing.

5. USPS HQ provides ZIP Code information to Point of Sale (POS) ONE retail systems nationwide via electronic download. (Not all post offices are on POS ONE retail system.)

6. USPS puts ZIP Code information in postal bulletins, which are published biweekly.

(b) It is only after postal assets arrive and post offices are established that the mail can begin to flow. The entire process from JRSOI of postal assets to start of mail flow could take up to 30 days to complete. Commanders must factor in both the JRSOI and ZIP Code request process when deciding when to request MPO/FPO addresses. However, commanders may upgrade postal priorities based on a changing operating environment.

(5) On or after C-day, or prior to C-day if JRSOI operations are continuous, initiate and/or process request for free mail. The GCC's postal staff submits the request through the GCC, who evaluates justification for compliance with Title 39, USC, Section 3401(a), and then forwards the action to the MPSA.

(6) Process requests for restrictions, including programs with theater-wide repercussions, such as mail embargoes or other restrictions, in coordination with the GCC's postal staff, and forward to the MPSA.

(7) Process and maintain all agreements or requests for exception to user policy for support to international military commands, other government agencies, and NGOs and forward through the GCC's postal staff to MPSA. Requests will be processed IAW the statutory requirements of Title 39, USC, Section 3401 (a).

(8) Ensure that regular, standardized reporting procedures are implemented for all MPOs and MPS activities, per guidance from MPSA. Provide regular consolidated reports on transportation and mail movement operations, terminal operations, mail volume, and backlogs, if applicable to the GCC's postal staff, Service component command postal managers, and MPSA.

(9) Coordinate and advise all postal contracting efforts by the Service component commands, and provide regular reports to the GCC's postal staff for review.

(10) Conduct staff assistance visits and inspections at all AOR MPAs. Assemble joint service teams when appropriate to enhance efficiency.

(11) Request the activation and deactivation of contingency ZIP Codes. The SPM is the sole authority for requesting, opening, or closing contingency MPOs.

(12) The base support installation will establish a postal box for units supporting DSCA operations within the US. The JTF J-1 or J-6 will coordinate for delivery of mail to personnel deployed within the JOA.

g. **Joint Forces Postal Staff.** The joint forces postal staff will implement all postal operations in the operational area, IAW CCMD guidance. The joint forces postal staff will perform the following tasks.

(1) Coordinate support, to include funding, for joint MPS theater hub facilities when activity support is not organic to the base or unit operating infrastructure (e.g., MCAs or AMTs at international airports).

(2) Coordinate the designation of a single-service postal manager (SSPM) to implement postal policies throughout the operational area. While primary responsibility for postal operations still resides with the joint forces postal staff, functional management of the theater MPS may be delegated to the single component command that maintains the postal activity with a capability best suited to coordinate joint postal matters.

(3) Coordinate for the establishment of a JPC for significant joint operations. Personnel augmentation for the JPC staff should consist of an SSPM core staff and be representative of the service force structure of the joint force. The JPC, when active, will operate under the guidance of, and assume responsibilities and authority from the SSPM. The JPC will coordinate postal operations in the joint force operational area and will perform the following CCMD J-1 actions:

(a) Coordinate MPS operations at all military postal activities MPOs, MCAs, AMTs, fleet mail centers, and surface mail terminals in the operational area.

(b) Establish, on request, additional postal restrictions or embargo procedures. This may be necessary if excessive mail volume is hampering the flow of mission-essential supplies and equipment into the operational area.

(c) Specify any restrictions for retrograde mail, to include size and weight limitations and security screening.

(d) Request free mail privileges IAW Title 39, USC 3401 (a), this publication, and DOD 4525.6-M, *Department of Defense Postal Manual,* if not previously requested.

(e) Identify, confirm, and maintain the operational area APOEs/SPOEs and APODs/SPODs.

(f) Ensure that individual Service components develop and maintain casualty mail procedures and directory services.

(g) Provide MPS PNAs, SITREPs, and transit time information.

(h) Act as POC for all operational area MPS-related queries, congressional inquiries, and service complaints.

(i) Publish uniform procedures applicable to all service MPS activities in the operational area.

(4) The GCC, based on a recommendation from the joint forces postal staff, may designate one of the component commands the responsibility to accomplish mail movement functions within the operational area. This designation will be selected based on their capabilities. More than one designee may be appointed for operational areas with distinct geographical areas or sectors, or for distinct operational responsibilities, such as surface, maritime, or air. Responsibilities for designees are outlined in DOD 4525.6-M, *Department of Defense Postal Manual,* or its replacement.

3. Planning Considerations and Execution Requirements

a. Commanders must consider postal support for various types of operating environments ranging from austere locations where infrastructure is nonexistent to robust locations where permanent facilities are available.

b. For operations of significant forces, or when designated, the GCC postal staff will establish a JPC or SPM for the joint force operational area.

c. The Service component commander designated the EA responsibility for air transportation and sorting will usually be the Air Force component commander. This responsibility includes management of AMTs and APOE/APOD MCAs.

d. The Service component commander designated the EA responsibility for land transportation and sorting will usually be the Army component commander. This responsibility includes management of JMMTs and land MCAs.

e. The JMMT should be large enough to facilitate mail volume equal to 2 pounds per Service member per day. This number does not take into consideration any Service member mail or future legislation providing resources that would allow family members to make qualified mailings free of postage. Legislative changes would require an increase in the planning factor.

f. The Service component commander designated the EA responsibility for maritime transportation and sorting will usually be the Navy component commander. This responsibility includes management of joint fleet mail centers (JFMCs) and surface port MCAs.

g. Service component commanders with units responsible for postal operations will provide trained clerks for joint MPS activities, such as JMMTs or AMTs. Commanders must determine how to flow postal personnel into theater to ensure the mail delivery system is in place once the JRSOI and APO request process is complete. The sourcing of trained personnel should be based on Service population, on a pro rata basis, determined by the following guidelines. Note: Population for Navy afloat units with organic postal operations and embarked Marine Corps personnel should not be considered for MPO and Postal Finance Office calculations.

(1) MPO: 1 trained clerk per 500 personnel during initial operations (30 days); 1 per 500 for sustainment operations up to 10,000 personnel; and 1 per additional 1,000 personnel thereafter.

(2) AMT/JFMC: 1 trained clerk per 1,500 personnel supported.

(3) Postal Finance Office: Minimum 2 personnel.

(4) Postal Volumes: Units can expect to process 2 pounds of mail per deployed Service member per day.

h. During the planning stages, commanders must ensure the availability of dedicated postal equipment and postal supplies necessary to start and maintain the flow of mail. Postal equipment includes dedicated trucks, containers, container handling equipment, forklifts, pallet jacks, and specialized postal equipment. Equipment should be integrated into the time-phased force and deployment list in time to support the timely flow of mail into the operational area. Services should ensure their logistic details or Service specific pre-pack inventories are periodically reviewed and updated. Pre-positioned assets should be specifically earmarked to support JMMT operations, and Service postal personnel should access, receive, and set up the pre-positioned assets necessary to conduct postal operations in theater. These factors apply to austere or robust operating environments.

i. Planners should refer to DODI 4525.7, *Military Postal Service and Related Service,* for planning factors when establishing a military mail terminal.

j. In general, the predominate component within the operational area will command the postal facility that serves its personnel. Facilities that perform a joint role (e.g., AMT, JMMT) will be the responsibility of the functional component commander.

k. Coordinate for letter-class mail (LCM) to receive Commodity 1 designation (Logistics Supply Class VI-M) for intertheater and intratheater transportation upon commencement of operations.

l. Service postal representatives should elevate problems and issues concerning conduct of postal operations to the GCC's postal staff via the SPM (if designated) using a SITREP.

m. Commanders must ensure that sufficient in-theater postal facilities exist to support postal operations. Planning factors must consider available existing infrastructure or lack of it to account for additional assets needed to include tents when permanent infrastructure is not available. These facilities must support the receipt, sorting, and distribution of mail. A discussion of facilities must also include adequate messing and billeting for postal personnel. Funding and asset acquisition are the responsibilities of the installation commander or base operating support service (BOSS) designated leasing agent for the use of organic assets.

(1) During the initial buildup of an initial contingency postal facility, military postal clerks may live within the postal facility as long as a secured door separates the living quarters and the MPO. Commanders will ensure that postal clerks are not permitted to have unescorted access to mail after normal duty hours. The only exception would be security-type personnel performing that specific duty.

(2) All facility design proposals will require approval by the GCC's postal staff or SPM, if designated, prior to engineering design completion and fund allocation. Basic facility designs or locally acquired existing buildings will adhere to or meet basic construction and security requirements outlined in the DOD 4525.6-M, *Department of Defense Postal Manual*. Initial contingency operations may require some temporary basic security waivers (approved by the theater-designated postal manager and local resource manager) until the resources are available (e.g., alarm systems).

(3) Commanders must also plan for and obtain rolling stock to adequately meet short- and long-term military postal service requirements.

(4) JMMTs. The basic working space is one square foot per two supported members. For instance, if the full-service JMMT provides support for five bases with a total combined population of 100,000 personnel, the facility's square footage would be calculated at an estimated 50,000 square feet. A full-service JMMT that provides service via ground and air and is a primary regional or country APOD will operate within the confines of the servicing active aircraft runway with full unrestricted access to arriving and departing aircraft for on- and off-loading purposes.

(5) MPOs. Fully operational post offices with all functions that include a MCA responsible for aircraft receipt and dispatch operations should have at least one square

foot per supported member. Activities should ensure unimpeded truck or container operating space.

(6) Rolling stock or automated equipment. The installation or responsible BOSS will provide adequate vehicle/surface mail transportation support, to include consideration for rough-terrain container handlers; 20- and 40-foot International Organization for Standardization containers; nontactical and tactical vehicles to transport postal clerks to and from work facilities; flat-bed trailers; tractors; 5- to 10-ton lockable body trucks; 5- to 10-ton forklifts; conveyor systems, etc.

n. Postal activities will use a pro-rata service postal clerk assignment allocation process to ensure fair workload representation based on the totality of populations served. The predominant component population for an installation or MPO service area will provide the postal leadership for that activity. Note: Personnel onboard Navy afloat units (including embarked personnel) served by organic postal operations are excluded from the calculations above.

o. The GCC must review and consider HN customs requirements and status-of-forces agreement/security agreement before establishing postal operations.

4. Levels of Service

a. Operations that do not exceed 30 days in duration will not usually initiate supporting mail service. However, joint force components may continue to provide organic unit service, and may expand service to support the entire joint force, if warranted and feasible.

b. Upon commencement of operations, mail may not be accorded priority of transport into, and within, the operational area due to critical personnel and other cargo considerations. The GCC designates a transportation priority for mail commensurate for the level of service desired (e.g., Priority 1 for LCM, and Priority 2 for parcels); or Priority 1 for both LCM and parcels. Failure to specifically accord priority to mail may result in delivery delays until alternate transportation resources are available (Civil Reserve Air Fleet, commercially contracted air, Air Mobility Command flights, etc.).

c. Dispatching postal activities will always separate LCM, in all stages of transportation, in a manner that allows easy retrieval if the shipment cannot move in its entirety. LCM will always move ahead of parcel mail, and all activities will take additional measures to ensure the oldest mail (received at the en route activity at the earliest date) is moved first. All postal activities will comply with command-directed ballot processing measures as soon as the GCC's postal staff or SPM, if designated, has published them.

5. Postal Restrictions

a. Commanders have high expectations for unrestricted postal services to enhance morale and communication. However, operational constraints such as rapidly moving units, or an overburdened logistic system, may require temporary postal restrictions to prevent backlogs of mail. The GCC's postal staff, in coordination with the MPSA, may recommend mailing restrictions for GCC approval if such constraints will not permit mail movement into and out of the operational area.

b. Commanders should consider the following mail restrictions during combat operations in order to avoid hampering the flow of mission essential supplies and equipment into the operational area:

(1) Restrict all mail for contingency ZIP Codes for the first 30 days.

(2) Allow LCM at 30-day point if JRSOI of postal equipment and personnel is complete and request for MPO address is submitted to MPSA and returned approved.

(3) Allow small parcels up to 5 pounds at 60-day point.

c. All restrictions should be removed after 90 days. To reduce the amount of frustrated mail, addresses should not be distributed until 30 days after postal units, equipment, and infrastructure is in place.

d. Additionally, a communication strategy should be developed to manage customer expectations of when letters and packages can be mailed to the theater.

e. Full postal services, such as postal money orders, express mail, and/or registered mail service, may not be offered in the initial or immediate sustainment phases of the operation due to the required infrastructure, security, and training associated with these services. Absence of these services should have negligible impact on morale.

6. Contracted Postal Services

a. During some operations, postal services may be contracted to reduce the military logistic infrastructure and/or personnel assigned to support functions. All contracted postal services must adhere to DOD and USPS regulations and MPS policy. Outsourcing should be accomplished IAW current DOD policies regarding use of foreign and local nationals. Any new contract or modifications and adjustments must be coordinated with the primary customer's Service postal representative, the GCC's J-1, J-6, SPM, or SSPM prior to execution.

b. The GCC's postal staff is responsible for managing AOR postal procedures and for coordinating with the Service component commands the criteria for contracted postal services in the theater. Additionally, the GCC's postal staff provides specific requirements within their AO for the contractor to the contracting command to ensure compliance with the specified statement of work/performance work statements and provisions within the actual contract.

c. The contracting or leasing of equipment, maintenance, and personnel should only be pursued if there are no USPS or military assets available to accomplish the mission.

7. Free Mail

a. Free mail is authorized by Executive Order 12556, *Mailing Privileges of Members of Armed Forces of the United States and of Friendly Foreign Nations,* and Title 39, USC, Section 3401(a). In 1986, the President delegated authority to SecDef to expedite implementation. Free mail is a privilege specifically granted by this law, and is intended solely to expedite transmission of military members' personal correspondence back to their families and friends in the US in times and places of war.

b. Free mail privileges apply to Service members in the designated operational area as well as those hospitalized in a facility under military jurisdiction as a result of service in the designated area. It also applies to civilians who are designated by the GCC as essential to and directly supporting the military operation, and will generally be limited to DOD employees and US citizen DOD CAAF and authorized non-CAAF of US owned and operated companies in direct support of the contingency and stationed in the operational area. See DOD 4525.6-M, *Department of Defense Postal Manual,* or its replacement for more information on DOD postal policy.

c. Free mail is limited by Title 39, USC, Section 3401 (a) to personal letter or sound recorded correspondence (to include videotapes) and must be addressed to a place within the delivery limits of the USPS or MPS. Free mail privileges are not normally allowed when mail is processed, handled, or delivered by a foreign postal administration. Examples of sound and video recorded correspondence include all media forms, such as camera film, video disks and memory cards, compact discs, digital video devices (DVDs), etc. Free mail privileges do not apply to DSCA operations within the US.

d. The GCC must request free mail for a specific area where the Armed Forces of the United States are:

(1) Engaged in action against an enemy of the US.

(2) Engaged in temporary military operations under arduous circumstances.

(3) Engaged in military operations involving armed conflict with a hostile foreign force.

(4) Serving with a friendly foreign force in an armed conflict in which the US is not a belligerent.

(5) Temporarily deployed overseas for an operational contingency in arduous circumstances. It should be noted that "morale and equity" is not a term used in the statute that governs free mail, and therefore that term cannot be used as a criterion for granting free mail privileges. In general, arduous circumstances are determined to be forward expeditionary areas where normal garrison support activities, specifically MPOs, are unavailable to provide postal services, such as the purchase of stamps. Request for free mail is submitted by electronic message Defense Message System (or signed memorandum via email) directly to the MPSA.

e. MPSA forwards the request with its recommendation to SecDef through the Assistant Deputy Under Secretary of Defense, Transportation Policy (ADUSD[TP]) and Deputy Under Secretary of Defense, Logistics and Material Readiness.

f. ADUSD(TP) coordinates with the DOD General Counsel to confirm that the request complies with the law. They coordinate with the Joint Staff J-1 and USD(P&R), for concurrence. Concurrently, they consult with DOS and the Postmaster General, USPS, on SecDef's intention to authorize free mail in the area requested.

g. When approved by SecDef, MPSA releases detailed implementing instructions to the GCC and USPS. Free mail is not considered authorized until the GCC has received official approval from SecDef.

h. Upon completion of the joint operation, the GCC requests termination of free mail via MPSA. GCCs must review and revalidate free mail areas annually to ensure that the conditions that authorized free mail are still applicable. GCCs must submit validation reports to MPSA no later than 1 September. MPSA must submit a consolidated free mail report to ADUSD(TP) no later than 1 October. In the absence of revalidation, SecDef may terminate a free mail authorization.

8. United Nations Operations

The UN is recognized as a formal postal administration. It has its own frank, as well as UN stamps, which are honored by the USPS. Postal service during UN operations is as follows:

a. The UN provides free mail service from the UN mission area to home countries for individual personnel of military contingents. This service includes both personal and official mail, which must be franked with the UN impression. The free mail service does not apply from home countries to contingents.

b. All official mail from contingents is delivered at the UN expense.

c. Only first class letters and post cards, weighing 10 grams or less, will be accepted as free mail from members of a contingent. Individual members are entitled to dispatch up to five free letters per week, including UN aerogrammes, which are provided at UN expense. UN aerogrammes constitute the bulk of personal correspondence. Individual contingents are allocated five aerogrammes per week. No enclosures are permitted in aerogrammes.

d. It is the responsibility of the UN mission post office to receive bundles of free mail franked with the UN impression by contingents, consolidate it in mail bags, and dispatch it to postal authorities in the respective home countries.

e. When significant US forces are deployed under the auspices of the UN, postal support for US Service members is normally a US responsibility.

f. When the US initiates military operations unilaterally, organic MPS support is always established. When US operations are transferred to UN control, MPS support will normally be continued for US forces.

9. Postal Support for Foreign Forces

a. Foreign military units serving with the Armed Forces of the United States, upon the request of their government, may be authorized to move closed mail to and from their home country through MPS channels when the international postal infrastructure is inadequate. This mail must be transported at the requesting countries' expense. Mail for foreign forces is subject to the same restrictions as those applied to US forces, and additional individual country restrictions may apply.

b. Requests for foreign postal support may be received from a variety of sources: diplomatic, foreign nation postal administration, foreign nation military, etc. However, the first military organization that receives the request must forward the request to the GCC's postal staff for coordination among MPSA, applicable military commands, and other government agencies.

c. GCCs should request SecDef approval to draft an implementing arrangement to an existing acquisition and cross-servicing agreement (ACSA) to authorize postal support, detail processes, and identify reimbursement arrangements for requesting partner nation forces to receive postal support through the MPS. Procedures for requesting MPS support for foreign forces via an ACSA are as follows:

(1) GCC completes the implementing arrangement postal template document (available from MPSA) as the official request. Coordination on both ends of the transportation lane is essential to ensure success, so the POC information in the attachments is critical. MPSA will assist with cost reimbursement data between the origin and destination.

(3) When drafted, GCC submits the implementing arrangement to MPSA.

(4) MPSA coordinates with USPS, OSD, Services, DFAS, and other GCCs as necessary and informs the requesting GCC of approval to proceed.

(5) GCC obtains the requesting country's ministry of defense signature and GCC's J-4 signature on the implementing arrangement, as approved by MPSA/OSD, and will implement the agreement.

(6) When implemented, the mail and reimbursement process includes the following steps:

(a) When the foreign country hands the closed bag of mail to the receiving MPO, the receiving MPO completes the standard form for reimbursement (included in the implementing arrangement template packet) and submits it to the component postal manager along with a copy of the AV-7 bill of lading document. The mail is routed and sent to the destination MPO for hand-off to the foreign nation military. This is done for both prograde and retrograde mail whenever a closed bag is handed to the MPO from the foreign military. The reimbursement form requires signatures from both parties.

(b) The Service component commands will submit the reimbursement form electronically to DFAS through the appropriate Service contact to start the reimbursement process.

(c) DFAS will bill the foreign government using established processes, receive the payment, and transfer the payment back to the Service submitting the reimbursement document using the fund cite annotated on the reimbursement form.

d. GCCs may use a memorandum of understand (MOU)/memorandum of agreement (MOA) arrangement only when an ACSA or other applicable treaty is arrangement not currently be in place. Procedures for requesting MPS support for foreign forces using an MOU or MOA are as follows:

(1) The GCC's postal staff evaluates the foreign government request in collaboration with legal counsel and makes appropriate recommendations to MPSA using an MOA.

(2) MPSA coordinates implementation with applicable agencies (e.g., USPS, Customs, DFAS) and notifies the GCC's postal staff upon completion.

(3) The GCC's postal staff contacts the senior US military liaison officer to ensure that the country agrees to pay transportation costs for its military mail. Billing procedures are established in the MOA prior to implementation.

(4) In cases in which the host country is located in an operational area of another GCC, coordination must be made among the joint forces postal staff of each applicable GCC.

(5) Upon approval by the foreign country, the GCC's joint forces postal staff coordinates start-up dates with MPSA. MPSA verifies the foreign government billing procedures prior to establishing a start-up date.

(6) MPSA secures OSD approval of the MOA and notifies the GCC of the start-up date.

e. Foreign forces have options other than requesting MPS support, which include using their own military postal system, international mail, direct air freight, or their country's diplomatic pouch systems.

10. Reporting Standards

a. The GCC's postal staff will determine SITREP reporting requirements for all Service component-controlled postal activities providing support for operations. SITREP reporting requirements should include the accountability and the serviceability of postal equipment and supplies.

b. Postal activities will transmit PNAs, per DOD 4525.6-M, *Department of Defense Postal Manual,* or its replacement, whenever mail transportation is disrupted or impacted significantly, to include security incidents and combat-related delays or losses.

c. For prolonged operations, postal activities should be visited and inspected at least annually by the Service component postal managers, GCC's postal staff, and/or SPM/JPC (if activated), prior to a postal unit rotation; or upon leadership change, in order to ensure compliance with policy and to provide additional training as required.

11. Detainee Operations

If approved by the GCC, the GCC's postal staff will be responsible for planning the procedures for establishing postal support for detainees in the AOR. The CDO is responsible for all detention facility and interrogation operations in the JOA and coordinates with GCC postal staff for guidance relating to postal support for detainees.

For additional information concerning detainee operations, see JP 3-63, Detainee Operations.

Intentionally Blank

APPENDIX K
MORALE, WELFARE, AND RECREATION

1. General

a. MWR programs are mission-essential to combat readiness. They contribute to successful military operations by promoting individual physical and mental fitness, morale, unit cohesion, and esprit de corps, and by alleviating mission-related stress. If direct combat is not imminent upon deployment of a joint force, then the rapid implementation of MWR programs will be all the more important.

b. From a joint perspective, MWR programs may include but are not limited to the following: fitness programs and recreation facilities, exchange and resale services, entertainment services (to include military band operations), food and beverage sales, book and video services, newspapers, access to telephones and other communication media, and R&R programs.

c. Family well-being impacts Service members' focus on the mission and is thus very important to sustained readiness. The family well-being of deployed US Service members is a Service responsibility. In the event of civil support operations, family assistance centers and/or emergency family assistance centers may be established to support families affected by man-made or natural disasters.

d. Based on the duration and scope of DSCA operations in the US, the base support installation may be directed to provide MWR activities for the supporting forces.

2. Planning and Execution

a. **Planning Considerations for Exchange Support**

(1) The key to successful exchange support is careful planning in both the deliberate planning and the CAP processes. Plans should identify required exchange activities and supporting resources (to include Army and Air Force Exchange Service [AAFES] and Marine Corps Exchange lift requirements and be included in the TPFDD. Funding for transportation of personnel, merchandise, facilities, fuel, and support equipment is provided by supported Service component commands. Component commanders are also responsible for providing support to exchange activities such as communications, finance support, security, and fire protection.

(2) There are three types of AAFES activities, all of which may be organized in support of a single military operation.

(a) Imprest Fund Activities. These are unit operated retail activities, normally used to support a deployment of short duration, or in support of small units in remote locations. Supported units are responsible for resupply.

(b) Mobile Field Exchange (MFE). An MFE is a military-operated retail activity with merchandise being supplied from a parent exchange. MFEs are employed in support of large tactical operations.

(c) Direct Operational Exchange–Tactical (DOX-T). A DOX-T is a civilian-operated retail activity. Personnel and merchandise are supplied from a parent exchange.

(3) Requests for exchange support from AAFES are forwarded to:

HQ AAFES, Attn: CS-C
P.O. Box 660202
Dallas, TX 75266-0202

Message Address: HQ AAFES DALLAS TX//CS-C//

(4) Requests for Marine Corps Exchange support are forwarded to the major command of the deployed unit, or to:

Commandant of the Marine Corps (MR)
Personnel and Family Readiness Division
3280 Russell Road
Quantico, VA 22134-5103

Message Address: CMC WASHINGTON DC MRA MR

(5) Deployed Navy and Marine forces aboard US Navy ships are supported by shipboard retail activities, vending operations, laundry, and dry cleaning facilities. If required, Navy ships store operations may be established ashore in the operational area. For other than expeditionary forces, requests should be forwarded to:

Commander, Navy Exchange Service Command
Code (CP)
3280 Virginia Beach Boulevard
Virginia Beach, VA 23452-5724

Message Address: NEXCOM NORFOLK VA//C//
DMS address
SMPT [simple mail protocol transport] address

(6) Requests for Coast Guard Exchange System support should be forwarded to:

Commanding Officer
Coast Guard Community Services Command
 Battlefield Technology Center 1
510 Independence Parkway, Suite 500, Chesapeake, VA 23320

Message Address: COGARD CSC CHESAPEAKE VA

b. **Initial MWR Support**

(1) Initial support is a Service responsibility and will be provided IAW the Service doctrine for initial deployments.

(2) Fitness and recreation may be considered the heart of the MWR program for joint operations. US military units will arrange for, or deploy with, a basic load of MWR equipment included in their organic fitness and recreation kits and an organizational MWR specialist and/or generalist, if assigned.

(3) The JFC is responsible for operation of fitness and recreation programs/facilities during initial deployment. At a minimum, units should be prepared to conduct unit-level sports programs, provide table games for self-directed or group activities, provide recreational reading materials, provide opportunities for individual fitness needs, and be prepared to operate activities that sell exchange retail merchandise.

(4) American (National) Red Cross (ARC) services are closely related morale activities requiring joint oversight and support.

(a) ARC provides services to active duty military, members of the RC, DOD and USCG civilians, and their families worldwide to assist them in preventing, preparing for, and coping with emergency situations and providing emergency notifications to deployed Service members.

(b) All requests for ARC personnel to accompany US forces into an operational area during military operations must be forwarded to:

Family and Morale, Welfare, and Recreation Command
ATTN: ACS Division
4700 King Street
Alexandria, VA 22302-4418

Message Address: CDRUSACFSC ALEXANDRIA VA//CFSC-SF//

The United States Army Community and Family Support Center (USACFSC) organization is the DOD EA for deployment of ARC personnel during these situations. USACFSC-SF (Army Community Service Division) is responsible for coordinating the deployment, on-site support, and redeployment for ARC personnel. Costs of transportation, training, and uniforms (except for those paid for by the Red Cross) will be borne initially by the Army. The Army may request reimbursement from the other Services for deploying ARC employees supporting their units and personnel.

(c) The requesting JFC is responsible for providing logistic and administrative support for ARC personnel.

c. **Follow-On MWR Support**

(1) For joint force deployments of extended duration, additional support in the form of Service-level MWR kits or commensurate equipment and supplies will be provided through Service-level channels or procured locally as available to support deployed forces. These kits may contain strength and aerobic conditioning fitness equipment, sports equipment, reading materials, video and board games, audiovisual materials, motion pictures, televisions, videocassette recorders, DVD players, computers in Internet cafes to support e-mail communication, and game tables (pool, ping-pong, and foosball).

(2) If warranted, and based on the scope and duration of the deployment, tactical field exchanges will be established. Imprest fund activities may still be required in forward-deployed areas.

d. **Sustained MWR Support**

(1) As the operation progresses, the GCC should expand the MWR program. Commercial telephone services, Internet services and connectivity, direct operation exchanges (to include food, beverage, and other exchange concessions), special entertainment events, recreation facilities, and education and library services beyond recreational reading may be organized and established. Entertainment bands with military members should be used to entertain personnel, especially in remote or less secure operational areas where civilian entertainers cannot be used.

(2) The joint force J-1 has the responsibility to organize component command support and identify external requirements to sustain and improve MWR operations on-site. A WG comprised of Service component representatives may be established to accomplish these tasks.

(3) Establishment of an R&R program for military and civilians.

(a) Recreation sites, such as resorts or unit recreation areas, may be designated at secure locations within the operational area. The GCC may designate a component commander(s) to administer these sites.

(b) Based on conditions in the operational area and the length of deployment, the JFC may request that the GCC establish a supporting R&R program. Upon approval of the request by OSD, the GCC will develop an R&R program IAW DODI 1327.06, *Leave and Liberty Policy and Procedures,* and relevant civilian guidance, and may designate a component command the responsibility for implementation.

(c) OSD approval of the GCC's program is required if one or more of the following conditions apply:

1. R&R leave is included in the program.

2. Transportation to and from the R&R area is to be provided on a space-required basis (government funded).

<u>3.</u> Travel time is not charged to the Service member's leave account.

(4) Armed Forces Entertainment (AFE) Program. The purpose of the AFE program is to provide free, quality, live, professional entertainment to Armed Forces of the United States personnel and their family members stationed overseas. Priority is given to remote and isolated locations, ships at sea, and contingency operations. The goal of the program is to lift the spirits and morale of troops and maintain their readiness and effectiveness while serving in defense of our country. While raising the morale of troops stationed overseas, the AFE program provides entertainers with an appreciation of the hardships troops endure and helps them serve as a vital link between those at home and those providing our national security.

(a) The Secretary of the Air Force, as the EA for coordinating overseas entertainment within the DOD, administers the AFE program within the Directorate of Services under the Deputy Chief of Staff for Manpower, Personnel, and Services as the AFE office. IAW DODI 1330.13, *Armed Forces Entertainment Program,* AFE is authorized direct communication with the United Service Organizations concerning the entertainment of Armed Forces of the United States overseas.

(b) Since entertainers participating in the AFE program perform without compensation, commanders at all levels are encouraged to provide maximum support allowed by law and extend every courtesy in return for the substantial contribution, which the entertainers make to the morale and welfare of Armed Forces personnel and their families overseas.

(c) Component and subordinate commanders collect, consolidate, and forward entertainment requirements submitted by their installation/site commanders.

(d) GCCs consolidate and forward entertainment requirements submitted by component and subordinate commanders within their AORs. Additionally, GCCs ensure resources are provided to ensure success of the AFE program and appoint country coordinators who are responsible to:

<u>1.</u> Request, plan, and manage entertainment tours in their country and facilitate information flow between site coordinators and the regional manager.

<u>2.</u> Collect and consolidate site itineraries to develop in-country draft and final tour itineraries.

<u>3.</u> Disseminate tour information to applicable locations.

<u>4.</u> Track and coordinate logistic support between performance sites.

<u>5.</u> Coordinate local military airlift, if necessary.

<u>6.</u> Request country clearance authorizations, as requested by the regional manager.

7. Secure entrance/exit visas, as requested by the regional manager.

8. Ensure site coordinators' marketing/advertising efforts are sufficient.

9. Collect, review, and submit site coordinator tour evaluations and photos to the regional manager no later than 10 days following tour completion date.

10. Advise regional manager of any specific tour concerns/issues.

(e) The JFC's concept and/or plan for MWR support should be consistent with the GCC's guidance. The supported GCC may designate a component commander the responsibility for administering MWR support. The MWR designee will be responsible for the following:

1. Make recommendations for tasking other component commands through the CCMD J-1. Once approval is granted, direct liaison may be authorized for the coordination of similar levels of support.

2. Provide, contract, or coordinate for military or civilian MWR personnel required.

(5) Serve as an advocate to acquire the transportation priority necessary to move equipment and personnel as required.

(6) Arrange for funding authority for equipment and personnel.

(7) Coordinate with applicable exchange service for support.

e. The following guidelines apply to all levels of joint contingency operations beyond initial deployment.

(1) The JFC will establish equitable MWR support policies for execution.

(2) The responsibility for MWR operations should include MWR support and control of all Service-provided MWR resources based on JFC guidance.

(3) In areas occupied by a single Service, that Service will provide MWR support to its own units.

(4) In areas with a majority of one Service and minor elements of another, the predominant Service will usually be responsible to provide MWR support to the other Service elements.

(5) In areas where major elements of more than one Service are located, the JFC designee will establish MWR services.

f. MWR support for contingency operations will be funded by Service component commands through appropriated funds. Nonappropriated funds (NAF) generated by

MWR activities at contingency sites may be used to supplement MWR programs on a nonreimbursable basis only when those expenditures directly benefit troops and in those rare instances where expenditures in contingency locations do not meet the criteria for direct support through appropriated funds. In all other cases, NAF generated by MWR activities may be used to supplement MWR programs through advanced funding or on a reimbursable basis under the MWR Utilization, Support and Accountability or Uniform Funding and Management Practice, as appropriate, authorized in DODI 1015.15, *Establishment, Management, and Control of Nonappropriated Fund Instrumentalities and Financial Management of Supporting Resources.* While NAF such as unit funds may be expended in conjunction with contingency operations, use of other NAF may not be desirable because there is currently no legal authority for reimbursement of NAF accounts.

g. Military bands are an important tool available to the JFC to entertain personnel engaged in operations. MWR personnel should actively include military bands in their entertainment programs, especially in remote or less secure areas where civilian entertainers cannot be utilized. The CCMD J-1 is responsible for ensuring MWR and military band activities are synchronized. The J-1 is also responsible for designating the senior US military bandmaster to perform additional duties as a staff band officer responsible for coordinating military band activities, and assisting with the synchronization of military band operations and MWR entertainment programs.

Intentionally Blank

APPENDIX L
CASUALTY OPERATIONS AND CASUALTY REPORTING

1. General

a. Casualty Operations. Casualty operations are a Title 10, USC, responsibility of the respective Services. Each Service casualty office provides adequate guidance and information for its respective Service to facilitate appropriate management of casualty operations requirements and provide timely and accurate NOK notification for its Service members. Service casualty procedures remain relatively consistent across the range of military operations. Casualty processing procedures of deployed DOD civilians and CAAF who become casualties will be the same as required for military personnel (see Figure L-1).

b. Casualty Reporting. Joint force J-1 casualty reporting requirements are based on GCC guidance to make the chain of command aware of status of forces and events under their purview. The intent is not to duplicate Service reporting procedures. The joint force J-1 casualty reporting process utilizes the OPREP 3 or other operational reporting means directed by the GCC to expeditiously convey information to chain of command leadership, to include the President and SecDef. Whatever communications channels are used, handlers of personal data associated with casualties must safeguard it closely to prevent inadvertent release of information to the public ahead of official notification of NOK. DOD policy is that no casualty information will be released to the media or the general public until 24 hours after the NOK have been notified. In the event of a multiple loss incident, the start time for the release to the media (24-hour period) will commence upon the notification of the last family member.

c. For casualty tracking, care must be taken to avoid double counting. By-name visibility at the J-1 level ensures casualty numbers are accurate, especially with regard to "return to duty" and "died of wounds received in action."

d. Casualty liaison teams should be appointed, either as a joint team under J-1 cognizance or overseen by a Service component with a joint mission, at each major medical treatment facility and mortuary affairs collection point. Communication must be available between the J-1 and the other Service components in order to relay updates. Due to the joint nature of such functions, training should be provided by the J-1. Equipment, transportation, and billeting of the teams must be planned for.

2. Responsibilities

The joint force J-1 must ensure that Service components adhere to Service reporting requirements, particularly when there is no Service personnel element assigned. The joint force J-1 is also responsible for ensuring the chain of command and the Joint Staff receive casualty information via OPREP 3 or other designated communication channels. Additional information on casualty reporting can be found in DODI 1300.18, *Department of Defense (DOD) Personnel Casualty Matters, Policies, and Procedures*.

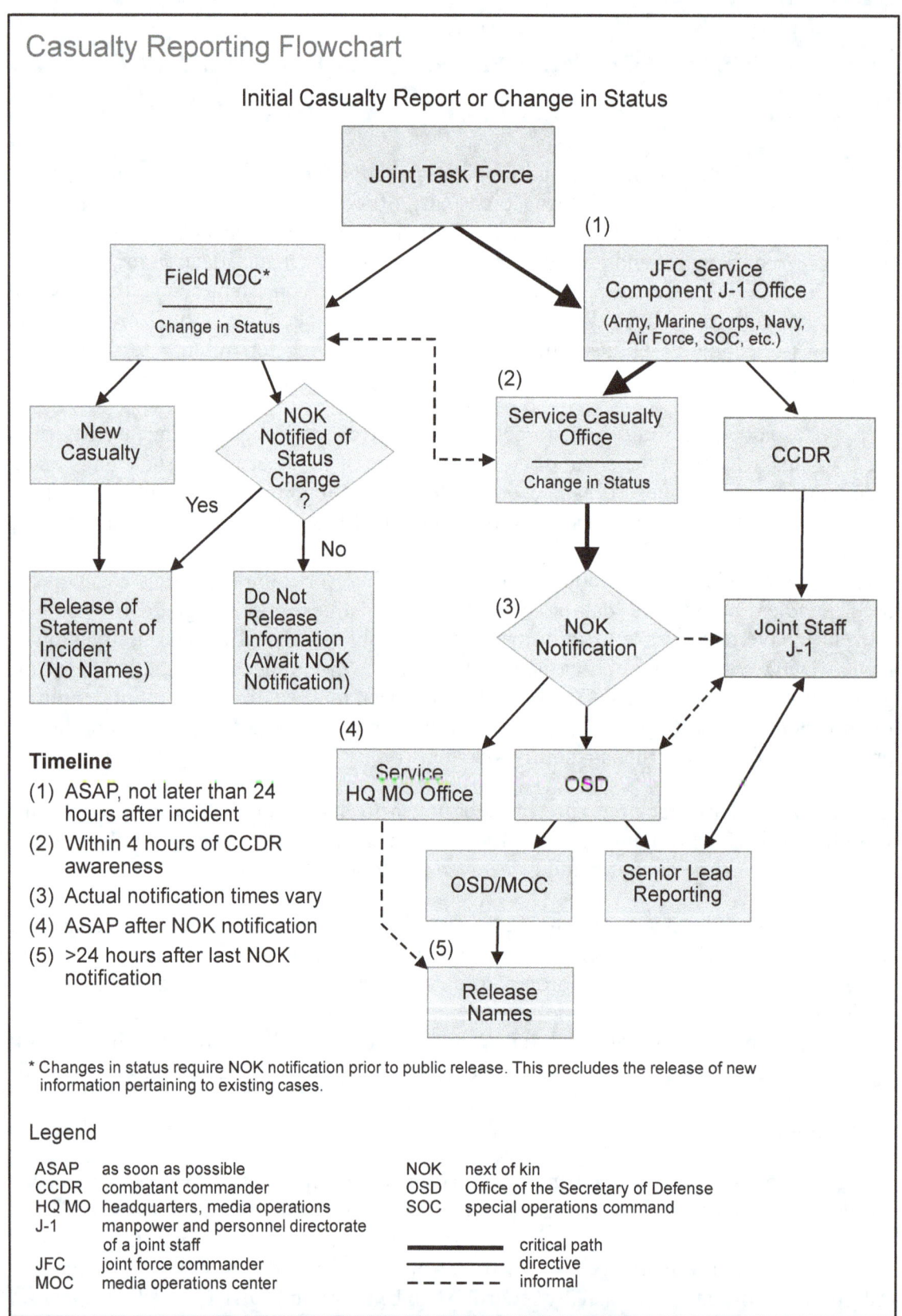

Figure L-1. Casualty Reporting Flowchart

3. Planning and Execution

a. Prior planning is essential to efficient casualty operations and reporting. When casualties occur, information must reach the right people as quickly as possible. The J-1 should possess appropriate Service directives and maintain POC at Service casualty centers in the event they must assist their components. Procedural mistakes in casualty reporting must not occur because they could potentially lead to NOK notification through the media, rather than through appropriate Service channels. Because NOK notification is a Service component responsibility, each Service component must ensure their rear detachment commanders have been trained appropriately on the casualty notification process. Military chaplains should advise commanders on religious support for the notification process and should be a member of the notification team (if available), but should not be detailed as the casualty notification officer.

b. Redundancy in reporting capability is an important planning consideration. Procedures should be in place to provide for off-site casualty reporting in the event the primary reporting section is unable to function. In operations or exercises with multiple deployment sites, personnel rosters should be shared among activities to provide this capability. For single site deployments, personnel rosters should be maintained at the next higher HQ.

Service Casualty Offices

ARMY: Personnel Contingency Cell
24 hours	DSN 225-9547
	(703) 695-9547
	(703) 697-9546
Fax	(703) 693-2408
E-mail	PCCIMA02@HQDA-AOC.army.pentagon.mil

NAVY: Navy Casualty Center
Duty hours	DSN 882-2501
	(901) 874-2501
24 hours	(800) 368-3202
Fax	DSN 882-6654
	(901) 874-6654
E-mail	MILL_NavyCasualty@navy.mil

AIR FORCE: AF Casualty Services Branch
24 hours	DSN 665-3505
	(210) 565-3505
	(800) 433-0048
Fax	DSN 665-2348
	(210) 565-2348
E-mail	AFPC.CASUALTY@randolph.af.mil

MARINES: USMC Casualty Branch
24 hours   DSN 278-9512
           (703) 784-9512
Toll-free   800-847-1597 Ext 1

Fax   DSN 278-4134
           (703) 784-4134
E-mail   casualty.section@usmc.mil

COAST GUARD: CG National Command Center
24 hours   (202) 372-2100
Fax   (202) 372-2925
E-mail   NCC@uscg.mil

APPENDIX M
AWARDS AND DECORATIONS

"The result of decorations works two ways. It makes the men who get them proud and determined to get more, and it makes the men who have not received them jealous and determined to get some in order to even up. It is the greatest thing we have for building a fighting heart."

General George S. Patton, Jr.
Portrait of Patton, 1955

1. General

a. The basic reference, DOD Manual 1348.33, Volumes I and II, *Manual of Military Decorations and Awards,* provides specific instructions regarding requesting and processing military decorations and awards. This section provides a synopsis of the information contained therein as it applies to joint operations. Refer to the basic reference for amplifying and specific information regarding award submission procedures and eligibility determination.

b. US Military Decorations and Awards. There are three general types of US military awards.

(1) Individual decorations recognize individual meritorious service or individual actions that demonstrate a degree of heroism or valor.

(a) Defense decorations for meritorious service appropriate for award to eligible members of joint activities include the humanitarian service medal (HSM), Joint Service Achievement Medal (JSAM), joint Service commendation medal (JSCM), Defense Meritorious Service Medal (DMSM), Defense Superior Service Medal (DSSM), and Defense Distinguished Service Medal (DDSM).

(b) The "V" device is authorized for the JSCM, if the citation is approved for valor (heroism) in a designated combat area. Service Secretaries retain authority to recognize heroic or valorous acts performed by members of their Services by award of the Army, Air Force, and Navy-Marine Corps Commendation and Achievement Medals; Air Medal; Soldier's Medal; Navy Marine Corps Medal; Airman's Medal; Purple Heart; Bronze Star; Distinguished Flying Cross; Silver Star; Army, Navy, and/or Air Force Cross; and Medal of Honor. That authority is retained by the Military Department Secretary regardless of the activity to which a Service member is assigned.

(2) Unit awards recognize an entire unit's meritorious service, heroism or valor. The Joint Meritorious Unit Award (JMUA), the only existing DOD unit award, recognizes the accomplishments of joint activities.

(3) Campaign medals (or theater awards) commemorate participation in wars and other significant US military actions.

(a) The Armed Forces Expeditionary Medal is a campaign medal awarded to members of the Armed Forces of the United States who participate in significant numbers within a prescribed area of operations in a designated US military operation during which they encounter foreign armed opposition or the imminent threat of hostilities.

(b) The Armed Forces Service Medal is a theater award presented to members of the Armed Forces of the United States who participate in significant peacekeeping or prolonged humanitarian operations.

(c) The Armed Forces Civilian Service Medal is a theater award presented to DOD civilians involved in direct support of the Armed Forces and who meet other specific criteria pertaining to the duration of the support in a specifically designated military operation beginning on or after 1 June 1992. Any eligible civilian employee who has been in the theater of operations and meets the other qualifying criteria is eligible for the award.

(d) Award of a campaign medal to an individual or unit requires participation in the action in the designated area of operation. Meritorious service or valorous or heroic acts may be recognized by the appropriate DOD or Service personal and/or unit awards. Award of a campaign-type medal does not preclude nor take the place of recognition of meritorious, valorous, or heroic service performed during an operation.

(e) Eligibility for campaign-type medals requires that the individual or unit be actually engaged in the operation, within specified geographic boundaries and time periods, and meet all other requirements of the specific award. Individuals and units supporting an operation from beyond the designated area of operations may be appropriately recognized for their contributions by personal and unit awards and Service campaign awards. Personnel may not receive two campaign-type awards for the same operation.

c. Foreign Decorations and Service Awards

(1) It is the policy of DOD that awards from foreign governments be accepted only in recognition of active combat service or for outstanding or unusually meritorious performance.

(2) Activities normally undertaken by the Armed Forces of the United States in support of an ally during peacetime are not considered sufficient to merit foreign individual or unit decorations.

(3) US military personnel are prohibited from requesting or encouraging the offer of an award or decoration from a foreign government.

d. Award of US Military Decorations and Awards to Foreign Military Personnel.

(1) DOD policy provides for the recognition of individual acts of heroism and achievement by Service members of friendly foreign nations when those acts have been of significant benefit to the US or have contributed significantly to the successful prosecution of a military campaign by the Armed Forces of the United States.

(a) Personal US decorations such as the Legion of Merit (in four degrees), Meritorious Service Medal, and a Military Department's Commendation Medal or Achievement Medal may be submitted to the respective Service for approval.

(b) Awards for heroic and valorous acts and for meritorious service in direct support of combat operations are authorized for foreign military personnel in ranks comparable to the grade of O-6 and below as delineated by the respective Service regulations.

(2) Currently, there are no US campaign and service medals authorized to be awarded to members of foreign military establishments.

2. Responsibilities

a. The CJCS shall:

(1) Approve award of the DSSM.

(2) Make recommendations to SecDef on requests for award of the DDSM and the Medal of Honor.

(3) Recommend to SecDef the establishment of new campaign medals when appropriate.

b. The DJS, shall:

(1) Adjudicate requests for award of the HSM and the JMUA.

(2) Adjudicate requests for personal DOD decoration exceptions to policy, and make recommendations to PDUSD(P&R) for blanket waivers of policy for specific operations or circumstances.

(3) Establish campaign medal eligibility and/or dates.

c. CCDRs shall:

(1) Adjudicate award of the DMSM, JSCM, and JSAM. (Approval authority for the JSCM may be delegated in writing to JTF commanders in the grade of O-7 or above. Approval authority for the JSAM may be delegated in writing to an officer in the grade of O-6 or above occupying an established command or staff position.)

(2) Submit JMUA and HSM recommendations to the DJS for joint units and activities under their command.

(3) Disapprove inappropriate requests for JMUAs.

(4) Provide recommendations to the DJS concerning campaign medal approval for specific operations, to include recommended area of operations and commencement and termination dates.

(5) Forward offers of personal foreign decorations to the Secretary of the individual Service member's parent Military Department for adjudication; forward offers of foreign unit, service, or campaign medals to the CJCS for processing by DOD.

(6) Request that the pertinent military counterintelligence organization conduct a background check and a counterintelligence records check in conjunction with the initiation of individual award recommendations for foreign military members.

(7) Forward to the Secretary of the Military Department concerned recommendations for award of that Military Department's Meritorious Service, Commendation, or Achievement Medal, and recommendations for award of the Silver Star, Distinguished Flying Cross, Bronze Star, Air Medal, Soldier's Medal, Navy and Marine Corps Medal, or Airman's Medal.

(8) Forward to SecDef, via the CJCS, all other proposals to award US Military Decorations to foreign nationals.

d. Subordinate JFCs shall:

(1) Submit timely recommendations and supporting information for individual, unit, and campaign awards to CCDRs.

(2) Forward offers of personal foreign decorations through the CCMD to the Secretary of the individual Service member's parent Military Department for adjudication.

e. Joint force J-1s shall:

(1) Initiate requests for award of the JMUA and HSM as appropriate.

(2) Determine eligibility for individual DOD decorations, the HSM, and the JMUA for individuals assigned to the joint force (make recommendations for individual exceptions to policy as appropriate).

(3) Ensure information concerning approved awards (HSM, JMUA, campaign medals) is disseminated to all elements under their command.

(4) Institute procedures to ensure documentation of approved awards is provided to members of the joint force prior to rotation from the operation or the disestablishment of the joint force.

(5) Communicate concerns regarding award issues to their commanders and/or the Joint Staff J-1 as they are identified.

3. Planning and Execution

a. The expeditious submission of requests for individual, unit, and campaign awards is key to ensuring timely recognition. The following are examples of actions that have contributed to delays in award adjudication during past operations.

(1) Withholding recommendations for valorous and heroic awards pending the outcome of requests for delegation of awarding authority to JFCs. Military Department Secretaries have rejected all such requests in the past.

(2) Withholding all recommendations for individual defense decorations for an operation pending the outcome of requests for "blanket" exceptions to policy affecting only a portion of the joint activity.

b. Communication is key; early requests for clarification of policy and notification of intent will prevent potential delay, downgrading, or disapproval of awards.

Intentionally Blank

APPENDIX N
PERFORMANCE REPORTING AND TRACKING

1. General

Service regulations vary on evaluation reports. Individual Services may have specific software that generates performance evaluation reports. The CCMD J-1 will provide guidance for the JTF J-1 on using specific software programs to generate evaluations. Reporting officials should document any joint matters duties in officers' evaluation reports. The following guidance ensures that all deployed personnel receive evaluation reports per appropriate Service reporting requirements.

2. Air Force

IAW Air Force Instruction (AFI) 36-2406, *Officer and Enlisted Evaluation Systems,* Letter of Evaluation (LOE) (AF Form 77) is optional for Air Force officers and enlisted personnel deployed for less than 120 days. However, to ensure deployment experience is documented, all Air Force personnel deployed for 60 days or more may receive an LOE by first-line supervisors. If desired at the time of deployment, the JTF J-1 will request a change of reporting official approval by the individual's unit command. Upon completion of deployment, the first-line supervisor will prepare an evaluation report where the airman was deployed. A performance report is not required unless an annual report is due. If a unit deploys, an LOE is not required if the member's first-line supervisor also deploys and remains the first-line supervisor. Refer to AFI 36-2406, paragraph 5.3, for further information, especially as it pertains to reports required in a combat zone. AFI 36-1001, *Managing the Civilian Performance Program*, is the authority for Department of the Air Force civilian government employees.

3. Army

IAW Army Regulation (AR) 623-3, Army officers and enlisted personnel deployed for more than 90 days will receive an evaluation report (Department of the Army [DA] Form 67-9 for officers and DA Form 2166-8 for enlisted) by home station supervisors, effective the day prior to deployment. Upon completion of deployment, the first-line supervisor will prepare an evaluation report where the soldier was deployed. When deployed as a unit, no report is required unless a change or event occurs to cause a requirement for one. AR 690-400, chapter 4302, *Total Army Performance Evaluation System*, is the authority for DA civilian government employees.

4. Navy

a. Per Bureau of Naval Personnel Instruction 1610.10, concurrent reports should be submitted for personnel on TAD to the JTF for periods of more than 3 months. Reports for shorter periods are optional. Concurrent reports normally are submitted on detachment of concurrent reporting senior and/or detachment of the individual, and also may be when periodic reports are due. Concurrent reports will not be accepted for file without the regular reporting senior's countersignature. The CJTF must sign fitness reports on officers, unless written approval to delegate reporting senior authority is granted by Navy Personnel Command. The CJTF may delegate reporting senior authority for enlisted reports with the following limitations:

(1) Delegation should be accomplished in a command instruction that designates delegated reporting seniors by billet.

(2) Reports on pay grade E-5 to E-9 must be signed by an O-4/GS 12 or above.

(3) Reports on E-4 and below must be signed by an E-7/GS 11 or higher.

b. When deployed as a unit, no report is required if the reporting senior also deploys. Secretary of the Navy Instruction 12430.4, *Department of the Navy Performance Management Programs*, and Department of the Navy Implementation Guidance 430-01 serve as the authority for Department of the Navy civilian government employees.

5. Marine Corps

IAW Marine Corps Order P1610.7F with Change 1, Marines deployed 31 days or longer receive a "To Temporary Duty (TD)" report from the reporting senior at the parent command. This report will cover the period from the last report to the day prior to deployment. Upon completion of deployment, the reporting senior at the command to which the Marine is assigned TD submits a "From Temporary Duty (FD)" report. The FD report must be observed, and must cover the period from the end date of the TD report to the day before detaching to return to the parent command. Early termination of TD requires an FD report with reason for termination identified in section I. Submit a not observed report only when the early termination absolutely prevents meaningful appraisal and is not a relief for cause. Termination for cause requires the appropriate processing and review. Reports on Marines in a TD status lasting 31 days or longer must be submitted for grade change and change of reporting senior. Annual reports also will be submitted during periods of TD lasting 6 months or longer. When deployed as a unit, no report is required. Department of the Navy Implementation Guidance 430-01 serves as the authority for Department of the Navy civilian government employees assigned to the Marine Corps.

6. Coast Guard

Coast Guard Personnel Manual, M1000.6A, Chapter 10.A (Officer) and 10.B (Enlisted) provide guidance on the Officer Evaluation System and procedures for submission of OERs and enlisted employee reviews (EERs).

a. Officer reports must be done on form CG-5310 (series). A concurrent OER is an OER submitted in addition to a regular or special OER (done by permanent command only). A concurrent report is always in addition to a regular or special OER and thus does not count for continuity. Concurrent reports are normally submitted when an officer is performing TAD away from a permanent station for a period of at least 60 consecutive days while being observed by a senior other than the reported-on officer's regular rating chain. The concurrent OER is normally written upon the detachment of the TAD officer and covers only the period of TAD. If the reporting officer is a non-USCG officer, the reviewer for the OER must be a USCG officer who will provide mandatory reviewer comments.

b. EERs for regular active duty members are completed by the member's permanent unit. IAW USCG Personnel Manual, M1000.6A, Article 10:B.5.b.2. The TDY unit should provide written supporting documentation for input in the member's next regular EER when a member completes TDY for any length of time. Information on EERs is available at http://cgweb.uscg.mil/g-w/psc/adv.htm, in the "Quick Reference" box at the top left of the Web page. The Web site also contains a link to copies of the CG-3788 evaluation forms, which may be printed and used as a work sheet for the TDY unit to submit to the enlisted members permanent command as input.

c. EERs for reserve member's TDY for 92 days or more at a unit other than their permanent duty station for active duty due to mobilization or short-term active duty for special work (ADSW), the TDY unit now has the responsibility to complete the regular scheduled EER on the member IAW ALCOAST 077/04. If the TDY period is less than 92 days, the TDY command sends documentation to the permanent unit for entry into the member's regular EER. When the TDY period exceeds 92 days, and it has been more than 92 days since the last EER, then the TDY command will complete a Memo EER. When submitting an EER for this reason, select the reason of "Memo" in the drop-down menu under the Employee Review tab. At commands where Direct Access for Coast Guard personnel is not accessible, units may submit signed CG-3788 evaluation forms to PPC-adv for manual input into the system. A link to these forms can be found in the Personnel and Pay Procedures manual Personnel Service Center Instruction M1000.2a. Any TDY period more than 140 days (long-term ADSW) at a unit other than the permanent duty station is considered a permanent change of station transfer.

7. Evaluation Period

TDY/TAD reporting dates normally will be used as the basis for evaluation report start dates. Exception: when a member fails to report at the required time, the actual reporting date will be used for evaluation purposes.

8. Evaluation Processing

Reports that do not require review, approval, or signature from the CCDR may be written, completed, and sent to the respective Service HQ by the JTF. Reports that require review, approval, or signature from the CCDR must be sent to the CCMD J-1 as a final copy free of errors. The combatant command J-1 will review the proposed report for accuracy and format, and will require all errors to be corrected prior to delivering the report to the required CCMD office. Copies of signed reports shall be provided to the individual reported on and be maintained by the reporting senior/senior rater IAW Service regulations. The JTF J-1 may maintain copies of all performance reports only if permitted by Service regulations.

9. Commander, Joint Task Force, Evaluation

The CCDR normally will rate the CJTF.

10. Commander, Joint Task Force, Ratings

a. Deputy CJTF and JTF Service component commanders normally will be rated by the CJTF.

b. The CJTF, through the JTF J-1, will establish rating schemes and chains for all other JTF personnel, with the exception of unit-deployed personnel. Rating schemes remain within the JTF and must follow the CCDR's guidance and applicable Service directives.

c. Reports for foreign officers are based on policies applicable to the nationality and branch of service.

APPENDIX O
CIVILIAN PERSONNEL MANAGEMENT

1. General

Planners must ensure DOD civilian government employees and US contractor personnel are considered in every aspect of deliberate planning and CAP, consistent with their noncombatant status. This includes evaluating the appropriate manpower mix (military, government, or contractor) necessary to accomplish the mission, considering trade-offs in risk, cost, and capability. Moreover, contracted support should be reviewed carefully by all stakeholders (including manpower authorities) to ensure compliance with restrictions on contracting inherently governmental functions that are imposed by US law, regulation, and policy, as well as restrictions that may be applicable based on international law and international agreements regarding the use of contractor personnel. Their support should be reviewed in light of sensitivities associated with placing civilians in positions that might be viewed as performing inherently military functions.

2. Responsibilities

a. A GCC's J-1 is the principal agent for coordinating and integrating manpower plans and procedures for civilian support of joint operations.

b. Heads of DOD agencies deploying/redeploying civilians in support of an operation will ensure their personnel are aware of the GCC requirements to process through an APOD/SPOD upon their arrival in theater or through an APOE/SPOE upon their departure from the theater.

c. The GCC will ensure civilian requirements are included during operation planning. GCCs will identify positions that may be filled by civilians. They will also issue JOA/AOR-specific guidance relative to the deployment of DOD civilian government employees and US contractor personnel into the AOR.

d. Component commanders will provide the necessary resources to support, train, clothe, equip, and sustain the civilian work force in the operational area.

e. Heads of DOD agencies and non-DOD agencies deploying civilians in support of the operation must coordinate all support requirements for their personnel with the GCC and meet JOA/AOR admissions requirements as established by the GCC and IAW DOD 4500.54-M, *Department of Defense Foreign Clearance Manual,* DODD 1404.10, *DOD Civilian Expeditionary Workforce,* DODD 1400.31, *DOD Civilian Work Force Contingency and Emergency Planning and Execution,* DODI 1400.32, *DOD Civilian Work Force Contingency and Emergency Planning Guidelines and Procedures,* and DODI 1100.22, *Policy and Procedures for Determining Workforce Mix.*

3. Planning Considerations

a. **Civilian Personnel Requirements.** The GCC, through component commanders, is responsible for identifying civilian personnel requirements and managing DOD-related civilian resources in the JOA/AOR. JOA/AOR civilian resources may be DOD civilians, CAAF, non-DOD US civilians (e.g., other federal employees, the Red Cross, and DOS contractors), or augmentation personnel provided through HN support agreements. DOD civilians and CAAF deployed in support of a contingency will receive advance training, at a minimum, in the following:

(1) Chemical, biological, radiological, and nuclear defense and/or annual refresher training.

(2) Provisions of the Geneva Conventions.

(3) Wear and appearance of uniforms.

(4) Uniform Code of Military Justice (UCMJ) and Code of Conduct.

(5) Weapons certifications and firearms safety (if authorized and eligible to carry a weapon).

(6) Basic first aid.

(7) PR training.

(8) Self aid.

(9) Buddy aid.

(10) Country/customs familiarization (if outside the continental US).

b. **JOA/AOR Admission Requirements.** The GCC will publish guidance outlining admission requirements for the AOR. This will include, but is not limited to, the requirement for passports and visas, collection of DNA samples, completion of the DD Form 93 for emergency contact information, all immunization requirements, policy on HIV testing, and information pertaining to any other customs or laws that may impact deployment eligibility.

c. **Central Processing Centers.** GCCs will identify processing requirements for all DOD civilians and CAAF deploying to their AOR. If a central processing site is established, civilians must process through the facility to ensure they receive the same processing, equipment, and training afforded military personnel supporting the operation. However, CAAF may deploy through a process that incorporates all the functions of a deployment center in lieu of processing through the central processing center, if such a process is designated in the contract. Specific requirements for deployment processing must comply with DODI 3020.41, *Contractor Personnel Authorized to Accompany the US Armed Forces,* and component and GCC requirements. All requests for exceptions to processing requirements must be approved by the supported GCC prior to deployment. Refer to Appendix G, "Joint Personnel Reception Center and Joint Personnel Training and Tracking Activities."

d. **DOD Civilian and Contractor Employee Accountability.** Component commanders must ensure that component DOD civilians and CAAF in the joint operational area process through APODs/SPODs and APOE/SPOEs and are recorded in their Service's deployment system. Civilian personnel will be included in JPERSTATs submitted to the Joint Staff.

e. **Pay and Compensation.** While deployed to the operational area, civilian employees will be paid their basic pay and other applicable pay, including premium pay (overtime, holiday pay, night differential, Sunday premium pay, and compensatory time). If applicable, civilians may also be entitled to certain allowances, the most common being foreign post differential (FPD) and danger pay allowance (DPA). Combat zone tax exclusion does not apply to civilian pay and allowances.

(1) **Foreign Post Differential.** FPD is additional compensation authorized (up to 35 percent of basic pay) when the environmental conditions in foreign areas differ substantially from CONUS conditions and additional compensation as a recruitment/retention incentive is warranted. If applicable, FPD will commence on the 43rd day after employees have been stationed for 42 days in the area where the FPD is authorized. FPD payments and rates are determined by the Secretary of State.

(2) **Danger Pay Allowance.** DPA is additional compensation granted to employees for service at designated danger pay posts. DPA payments and rates are determined by DOS. If applicable, DPA (up to 35 percent of basic pay) commences on the date of arrival in the operational area, if already designated by the Secretary of State, or the date of designation if not already designated.

(3) **Additional Pay/Allowances.** The Office of Personnel Management and DOS will determine and establish any additional pay, compensation, applicable allowances and associated implementing guidance as a result of the contingency operation. The joint force J-1 is responsible for coordinating such action with the employee's parent Service personnel office and must ensure the pay and/or compensation needs of DOD civilians are met just as they are for the military force. This will include the initiation or validation of documentation to substantiate the request or claim.

f. **Identification and Geneva Convention Cards.** Servicing DEERS/Real-Time Automated Personnel Identification System facilities will issue a CAC, or appropriate identification, for the purpose of Geneva Convention identification to deploying civilians to include CAAF personnel prior to deployment IAW DODI 1000.1, *Identity Cards Required by the Geneva Conventions.*

g. **Casualty and Mortuary Affairs.** Casualty reporting and processing procedures for deployed DOD civilian employees will be the same as required for military personnel. Casualty and mortuary affairs reporting and processing for contractor personnel will be IAW DOD and GCC policy. See JP 4-06, *Mortuary Affairs.*

h. **Clothing, Equipping, and Training.** GCCs will identify JOA/AOR-specific clothing, individual equipment, and training required for civilian employees deploying to the operational area. Generally, commanders should not issue military garments to contingency contractor personnel or allow the wearing of military or military look-alike uniforms. When commanders issue any type of standard uniform item to contingency contractor personnel, care must be taken to ensure, consistent with force protection measures, that the contractor personnel be distinguishable from military personnel through the use of distinctively colored patches, armbands, or headgear. Generally, contractors are required to provide all life, mission, and administrative support to employees to perform the contract. When necessary, and as determined by the CCDR guidance, contingency contractor personnel may be issued military individual protective equipment (e.g., chemical defensive gear, body armor, personal protective equipment) subject to DOD policy, regulations, and contract terms. See DODI 3020.41, *Contractor Personnel Authorized to Accompany the US Armed Forces,* for more details. Training will include at a minimum the law of war, standards of conduct, UCMJ, antiterrorism, force protection, cultural and geographic orientation, and all safety-related training provided military personnel.

i. **Awards.** Awards for DOD civilians will be processed through their assigned Service personnel offices in coordination with the joint force J-1. DOD civilian employees in support of joint operations may be eligible to receive monetary and Service-specific honorary awards. DOD civilian employees assigned to joint organizations may be eligible for civilian awards. Monetary and Service-specific awards will be processed through assigned Service personnel offices in coordination with the joint force J-1. CJCS awards will be processed through the JTF J-1.

j. **Secretary of Defense Medal for the Defense of Freedom.** The Secretary of Defense Medal for the Defense of Freedom shall be awarded to any DOD civilian employee including employees of non-appropriated fund activities, when killed or wounded by hostile action while serving under any competent authority of DOD under conditions for which a military member would be eligible for receipt of the Purple Heart. SecDef has discretionary authority to award this medal to non-DOD personnel who are otherwise qualified to be awarded the medal based on their involvement in DOD activities. A civilian meeting the definition of "employee" under Title 5, USC, Section 2105, and who is eligible for an award under DOD 1400.25-M, Subchapter 451, may receive this award. CAAF are not eligible.

k. **Support and Services**

(1) **DOD Civilians.** DOD civilians deployed for military operations will be provided the same support and services provided their military counterparts. CCDRs will provide lodging, meals, security, postal support, and medical and dental care, except when specifically precluded by statute. DOD civilians are entitled to use exchange, commissary, and morale and welfare facilities while deployed. DOD civilians may be issued weapons for their personal defense and are not authorized to possess or carry personally owned firearms or ammunition. The issuance of weapons to civilian employees is contingent upon the approval of the CCDR and subject to CCDR guidance. Acceptance of weapons by civilian employees is voluntary, and in the case of CAAF, must also be approved by the employee's company. Upon acceptance, civilian

employees will adhere to military regulations regarding training, accountability, and safe handling of firearms. **Completion of weapons** training and certification **does not constitute** approval for carrying a weapon.

(2) **Contingency Contractor Personnel.** Based on DOD component consultation with the supported GCC and Defense Federal Acquisition Regulation Supplement requirements, DOD contracts providing contingency contractor personnel will contain language describing the specific support relationship between the contractor and DOD, including protection, authorized levels of health service, and other support and sustainment requirements. Generally, defense contractors are responsible for providing for their own logistic support and logistic support for their employees. However, logistic support shall be provided by DOD when the commander or the contracting officer determines provision of such support is needed to ensure continuation of essential contractor services and adequate support cannot be obtained by the contractor from other sources. See DODI 3020.41, *Contractor Personnel Authorized to Accompany the US Armed Forces*, for details. Contingency contractor personnel are not authorized to possess or carry personally owned firearms or ammunition or be armed during contingency operations unless specifically authorized (case-by-case basis) by the GCC or a designee no lower than the general or flag officer level or civilian equivalent. When armed, contingency CAAF may be armed to provide security services for other than uniquely military functions. In those cases, the geographic CCDR will issue written authorization identifying who is authorized to be armed and limits on the use of force. All requests to arm contractor personnel must follow specific DOD policy and procedures concerning the arming of contractor personnel given in DODI 3020.41, *Contractor Personnel Authorized to Accompany the US Armed Forces*.

(3) **DOD Civilian Expeditionary Workforce.** The DOD Civilian Expeditionary Workforce is a pre-identified group of DOD civilian employees trained and equipped to facilitate the use of their capabilities for operational requirements away from their normal work locations. Members of the DOD Civilian Expeditionary Workforce are trained and cleared to support combat operations by the military; contingencies; emergency operations; humanitarian missions; disaster relief; restoration of order in civil disorders; drug interdiction; and security, stability, and reconstruction missions of the DOD, when such support may appropriately be provided by DOD civilian employees. It is DOD policy to rely on a mix of capable military members and DOD civilian employees to meet DOD global security mission requirements. DOD civilian employees are an integral part of the total force. Commanders of CCMDs will ensure all operational plans, JMDs, and individual augmentee requirements incorporate support by DOD civilian employees.

Intentionally Blank

APPENDIX P
LANGUAGE AND REGIONAL EXPERTISE MANAGEMENT

1. Background

Language, regional expertise, and cultural awareness skills are vital enablers to joint operations. Since language and regional experts play a critical role in day-to-day operation, they are considered high-value targets by the adversary; therefore, care must be taken when considering force protection and operations security (OPSEC). Language and regional expertise skills can save lives and ensure mission accomplishment throughout confrontation, conflict, and stabilization operations.

2. General

Planners must ensure that language and regional expertise requirements are considered in every aspect of crisis, contingency, security cooperation, and humanitarian planning and day-to-day manning needs in support of military operations. This step includes evaluating the appropriate manpower mix (military, government, or contractor) necessary to accomplish the mission, considering trade-offs in risk, cost, and capability. Moreover, contracted support for language and regional expertise shortfalls should be reviewed carefully by all stakeholders (including manpower authorities) to ensure compliance with restrictions on contracting inherently governmental functions that are imposed by US law, regulation, and policy, as well as restrictions that may be applicable based on international law and international agreements regarding the use of contractor personnel.

3. Responsibilities

a. Senior language authorities understand the totality of the organization's language and regional expertise needs. They maintain visibility over all of the efforts related to language, culture, and regional expertise within their organizations and are members of the Defense Language Steering Committee IAW DODD 5160.41E, *Defense Language Program*, and DODI 5160.70, *Management of DOD Language and Regional Proficiency Capabilities*.

b. CCDRs ensure that language and regional expertise requirements are included during the developmental and implementation phases of operation planning, and language and regional expertise requirements are considered in every aspect of contingency, crisis, security cooperation, and humanitarian planning IAW DODD 5160.41E, *Defense Language Program*; CJCSI 3126.01, *Language and Regional Expertise Planning*; and DODI 5160.70, *Management of DOD Language and Regional Proficiency Capabilities*. They will also issue specific guidance relative to the deployment of language and regional expertise resources into an AOR.

c. CCMD senior language authorities identify, consolidate, track, and manage all foreign language expertise requirements for their geographic regions (less SOF). The USSOCOM senior language authority identifies, consolidates, tracks, and manages all

SOF foreign language and regional expertise requirements on behalf of all of the geographic CCMDs. CCMDs will periodically report foreign language and regional proficiency requirements IAW CJCSI 3126.01, *Language and Regional Expertise Planning.*

d. Joint Staff J-31, as the primary joint force coordinator, provides a joint sourcing solution recommendation for conventional force requirements to the GFMB IAW CJCSI 3126.01, *Language and Regional Expertise Planning.*

e. Component commanders will provide the necessary resources to support, train, clothe, equip, transport, and sustain the language and regional expert workforce in the operational area.

f. Heads of DOD agencies and non-DOD agencies deploying language and regional expertise resources in support of an operation must coordinate all support requirements for their personnel with the JFC and meet JOA/AOR admissions requirements as established by the GCC and IAW DOD 4500.54-M, *Department of Defense Foreign Clearance Manual;* DODD 1400.31, *DOD Civilian Work Force Contingency and Emergency Planning and Execution;* DODI 1400.32, *DOD Civilian Work Force Contingency and Emergency Planning Guidelines and Procedures;* and DODI 1100.22, *Policy and Procedures for Determining Workforce Mix.* They will also conduct periodic reviews and reports of their language and regional expertise programs IAW DODD 5160.41E, *Defense Language Program;* DODD 1315.17 *Military Department Foreign Area Officer (FAO) Programs;* CJCSI 3126.01, *Language and Regional Expertise Planning;* and DODI 5160.70, *Management of DOD Language and Regional Proficiency Capabilities.*

g. The Secretary of the Army will serve as the EA for all contract language and regional experts for DOD components, except personal services contract established by in-theater personnel, intelligence, and counterintelligence or USSOCOM IAW DODD 5160.41E, *Defense Language Program.*

4. **Planning Considerations**

a. **JOA/AOR Language and Regional Expertise Requirements.** The GCC, through component commanders, is responsible for identifying language and regional expertise requirements and managing DOD-related language and regional expertise requirements in the JOA/AOR. The CCMD senior language authority will support this effort. When requirements cannot be filled by military personnel, they may be filled by DOD civilians, CAAF, non-DOD US civilians (e.g., other federal employees, the Red Cross, and DOS contractors), or augmentation personnel provided through HN support agreements.

b. **JOA/AOR Admission Requirements.** In coordination with the GCC, the JFC will coordinate the approval and JOA/AOR admission requirements for all language and regional expertise resources being deployed to the operational area IAW the Foreign

Clearance Guide. The GCC will publish guidance outlining admission requirements for the operational area.

5. Clothing, Equipping, and Training Civilian and Contract Language and Regional Experts

GCCs will identify JOA/AOR-specific clothing, individual equipment, and training required for all language and regional expertise resources to include all military, civilian, and CAAF deploying to the operational area.

a. Generally, commanders should consider the safety of all personnel, including civilian and CAAF, performing on military facilities. CAAF are only allowed to wear uniform items specifically authorized in writing by the GCC and must carry such authorization with them at all times. When commanders issue any type of standard uniform item to CAAF, care must be taken to ensure consistency with force protection and OPSEC measures.

b. Generally, contractors are required to provide all life, mission, and administrative support to employees to perform the contract. When necessary, and as determined by the GCC guidance, CAAF may be issued military individual protective equipment (e.g., chemical defensive gear, body armor, personal protective equipment) subject to DOD policy, regulations, and contract terms. See DODI 3020.41, *Contractor Personnel Authorized to Accompany the US Armed Forces,* for more details.

c. Training requirement for civilians and CAAF will include the law of war, standards of conduct, UCMJ, antiterrorism, force protection, cultural and geographic orientation, and all safety-related training provided military personnel.

Intentionally Blank

APPENDIX Q
PERSONNEL SUPPORT TO MULTINATIONAL OPERATIONS

1. General

a. Multinational operations is a term describing military actions conducted by forces of two or more nations, typically organized within the structure of a coalition or alliance. An alliance is the relationship that results from a formal agreement between two or more nations to meet broad, long-term objectives (e.g., NATO). A coalition is an ad hoc arrangement between two or more nations or between alliances and nations for a common purpose.

b. Military operations have evolved beyond the traditional actions of deterrence and warfighting and now include peacekeeping, humanitarian assistance, and others. Actions of these types necessarily involve IGOs in the management of future crises and contingency operations. To accomplish these missions, the Armed Services must be prepared to operate in a multinational environment.

c. Personnel support for multinational operations remains a national responsibility.

d. CCDRs and subordinate JFCs should establish a status-of-forces agreement, MOA, and/or MOU regarding PR support between members of any alliance and/or coalition prior to the onset of operations.

2. United Nations Operations

Specific considerations for UN operations are addressed below.

a. **General.** Personnel support for US operations associated with the UN is complicated by a variety of factors. Lines of authority, responsibilities, command relationships, and reporting channels may become even more blurred with the introduction of multinational NGOs such as international health organizations. In this regard, the development of clear and defined terms of reference (TORs) is critical. These TORs must be proposed by the JFC or the CJCS and accepted by the UN command. The TOR must specify the relationship of US Service members to the UN (Foreign Assistance Act, United Nations Participation Act, and other appropriate areas) and their eligibility for UN awards and entitlements. CJCS deployment orders establishing command and control relationships for US personnel relative to UN control will be IAW the TOR.

b. **Process for Individual Personnel Requirements.** Refer to Appendix F, "Individual Augmentation Planning and Procedures," for the process to requisition individuals to fill UN positions associated with an operational requirement.

c. **Personnel Reporting Procedures.** Personnel accountability is both a UN and US national responsibility. Personnel assigned to UN duty are accounted for by the personnel reporting systems of the UN and that of their parent US Service. In addition to daily US strength reporting requirements, the UN may require a daily strength report of US personnel assigned to the UN for duty in order to reimburse the USG for its services.

It is important that the JFC monitor the status of personnel supporting UN operations in the area and/or JOA, as the JFC may be tasked to provide administrative support not provided by the UN.

    d. **Emoluments (Entitlements) and Awards.** Eligibility for UN awards and entitlements must be decided at the start of the operation. This eligibility should be included in the TOR.

        (1) UN Awards. The Secretary General of the United Nations establishes which UN operations qualify for UN awards as well as criteria for eligibility.

        (2) UN Emoluments (Entitlements). SecDef must approve eligibility of US personnel for UN entitlements. Examples of UN entitlements are UN leave and UN pay. Refer to Appendix H, "Military Pay, Allowances, and Entitlements," for information regarding UN emoluments.

3. North Atlantic Treaty Organization Operations

    NATO is one of the most successful military and political alliances in history. Its members have attained a level of interoperability unmatched in any other multinational military organization. This high level of interoperability is widely regarded as a model for future multinational contingency operations. Specific considerations for NATO operations are addressed below.

    a. **Commander, United States European Command's (CDRUSEUCOM's), Role in NATO Operations.** CDRUSEUCOM has dual responsibilities in NATO operations. First, CDRUSEUCOM commands all US forces dedicated to the operation if it is conducted in the United States European Command (USEUCOM) AOR. CDRUSEUCOM is aided in this capacity by the joint US staff at HQ USEUCOM. Second, in the primary role as Supreme Allied Commander, Europe, he commands all NATO forces and is aided in this capacity by an international staff at Supreme Headquarters Allied Powers, Europe (SHAPE). It is important to distinguish between these two functions performed by the same person. The US military personnel assigned to the SHAPE staff have been transferred from US national to NATO control and are NATO assets not governed by CDRUSEUCOM. US personnel contributions to NATO are preplanned and coordinated for operations approved by the North Atlantic Council. For nontraditional or contingency operations, US contributions must be carefully defined based on the mission. For NATO operations conducted outside of the traditional NATO/USEUCOM geographic area, the supported CCDR will normally exercise OPCON over US forces involved in NATO operations. For example, Commander, US Central Command, exercises OPCON over US forces assigned to NATO's International Security Assistance Force in Afghanistan.

    b. **Process for Requisitioning Personnel**

        (1) Authority to transfer US personnel from national to NATO control resides with the President and/or SecDef through the CJCS. The process for this transfer of control is outlined below.

(a) Request from NATO commander to United States National Military Representative (USNMR).

(b) Forwarding of request from USNMR to DOD.

(c) Transfer of control approved by OSD. The CJCS executes a deployment order to the appropriate force provider. Refer to Appendix F, "Individual Augmentation Planning and Procedures."

(2) When engaged in or providing personnel support to a NATO operation, CDRUSEUCOM may find that some personnel assets critical to the mission are not available from the Service components in theater. Under these circumstances, CDRUSEUCOM may wish to request temporary control of selected US personnel assigned to NATO. This control is for a finite period, after which the US personnel revert to their NATO billets. Return of US personnel from NATO to US control is coordinated through the USNMR to the NATO commander. The process for this transfer is outlined below.

(a) CDRUSEUCOM submits request to USNMR.

(b) USNMR forwards request to appropriate NATO commander.

(c) Upon approval of the NATO commander, USNMR requests the appropriate Service element at HQ SHAPE release the Service member to CDRUSEUCOM control.

Intentionally Blank

APPENDIX R
REFERENCES

The development of JP 1-0 is based upon the following primary references:

1. General

a. Title 5, USC, *Government Organization and Employees.*

b. Title 10, USC, *Armed Forces.*

c. Title 26, USC, *Internal Revenue Code.*

d. Title 37, USC, *Pay and Allowances of the Uniformed Services.*

e. Title 39, USC, *Postal Service.*

f. Title 41, USC, *Public Contracts.*

g. Title 42, USC, *The Public Health and Welfare.*

h. Mail Standards of the United States Postal Service, Domestic Mail Manual, http://pe.usps.com.

i. Executive Order 11157, *Regulations Relating to Incentive Pay, Special Pay, and Allowances.*

j. Executive Order 12556, *Mailing Privileges of Members of Armed Forces of the United States and of Friendly Foreign Nations.*

k. Executive Order 12656, *Assignment of Emergency Preparedness Responsibilities.*

l. National Defense Authorization Act for Fiscal Year 2004.

2. Department of Defense

a. DOD 1348.33-M, *Manual of Military Decorations and Awards.*

b. DOD 4500.54-M, *Department of Defense Foreign Clearance Manual.*

c. DOD 4525.6-C, *DOD Postal Supply Catalog.*

d. DOD 4525.6-M, *Department of Defense Postal Manual.*

e. DOD 7000.14-R, *Department of Defense Financial Management Regulations (FMRS),* Volumes 1–15.

f. DODD 1000.21, *DOD Passport and Passport Agent Services.*

g. DODD 1235.10, *Activation, Mobilization, and Demobilization of the Ready Reserve.*

h. DODD 1300.22, *Mortuary Affairs Policy.*

i. DODD 1400.31, *DOD Civilian Work Force Contingency and Emergency Planning and Execution.*

j. DODD 1404.10, *DOD Civilian Expeditionary Workforce.*

k. DODD 2000.12, *DOD Antiterrorism (AT) Program.*

l. DODD 2310.01E, *The Department of Defense Detainee Program.*

m. DODD 3002.01E, *Personnel Recovery in the Department of Defense.*

n. DODD 3020.49, *Orchestrating, Synchronizing, and Integrating Program Management of Contingency Acquisition Planning and Its Operational Execution.*

o. DODD 3025.14, *Protection and Evacuation of US Citizens and Designated Aliens in Danger Areas Abroad (*Short title: *Noncombatant Evacuation Operations).*

p. DODD 4500.54, *DOD Foreign Clearance Program (FCP).*

q. DODD 5100.01, *Functions of the Department of Defense and Its Major Components.*

r. DODD 5101.11, *DOD Executive Agent for the Military Postal Service (MPS).*

s. DODD 6495.01, *Sexual Assault Prevention and Response (SAPR) Program.*

t. DODI 1000.1, *Identity Cards Required by the Geneva Conventions.*

u. DODI 1000.13, *Identification (ID) Cards for Members of the Uniformed Services, Their Dependents, and Other Eligible Individuals.*

v. DODI 1215.06, *Uniform Reserve, Training, and Retirement Categories.*

w. DODI 1235.12, *Accessing the Reserve Components.*

x. DODI 1300.18, *Department of Defense (DOD) Personnel Casualty Matters, Policies, and Procedures.*

y. DODI 1327.06, *Leave and Liberty Policy and Procedures.*

z. DODI 1330.13, *Armed Forces Entertainment Program.*

aa. DODI 1340.09, *Hostile Fire Pay and Imminent Danger Pay.*

bb. DODI 1400.32, *DOD Civilian Work Force Contingency and Emergency Planning Guidelines and Procedures.*

cc. DODI 2200.01, *Combating Trafficking in Persons (CTIP).*

dd. DODI 3020.41, *Contractor Personnel Authorized to Accompany the US Armed Forces.*

ee. DODI 3001.02, *Personnel Accountability in Conjunction With Natural or Manmade Disasters.*

ff. DODI 4525.7, *Military Postal Service and Related Services.*

gg. DODI 6490.03, *Deployment Health.*

hh. DODI 6495.02, *Sexual Assault Prevention and Response Program Procedures.*

ii. Joint Federal Travel Regulation (JFTR).

3. Chairman of the Joint Chiefs of Staff

a. JP 1-02, *Department of Defense Dictionary of Military and Associated Terms.*

b. JP 1-05, *Religious Affairs in Joint Operations.*

c. JP 1-06, *Financial Management Support in Joint Operations.*

d. JP 2-0, *Joint Intelligence.*

e. JP 3-0, *Joint Operations.*

f. JP 3-16, *Multinational Operations.*

g. JP 3-33, *Joint Task Force Headquarters.*

h. JP 3-50, *Personnel Recovery.*

i. JP 3-61, *Public Affairs.*

j. JP 3-63, *Detainee Operations.*

k. JP 3-68, *Noncombatant Evacuation Operations.*

l. JP 4-0, *Joint Logistics.*

m. JP 4-02, *Health Service Support.*

n. JP 4-05, *Joint Mobilization Planning.*

o. JP 4-06, *Mortuary Affairs.*

p. CJCSI 1001.01, *Joint Manpower and Personnel Program.*

q. CJCSI 1301.01C, *Joint Individual Augmentation Procedures.*

r. CJCSI 3126.01, *Language and Regional Expertise Planning.*

s. CJCSI 3290.01B, *Program for Detainee Operations.*

t. CJCSI 5120.02B, *Joint Doctrine Development System.*

u. CJCSM 3122.01A, *Joint Operation Planning and Execution System (JOPES),* Volume I (*Planning Policies and Procedures*).

v. CJCSM 3122.03C, *Joint Operation Planning and Execution System,* Volume II (*Planning Formats*).

w. CJCSM 3150.13C, *Joint Reporting Structure—Personnel Manual.*

4. Service Publications

a. Department of the Army 36526, *Human Resources Doctrine.*

b. US Army Publication, *Joint Plan for DOD Noncombatant Evacuation and Repatriation (Non-Emergency).*

c. AFI 34-126(I), *Armed Forces Entertainment Program.*

APPENDIX S
ADMINISTRATIVE INSTRUCTIONS

1. User Comments

Users in the field are highly encouraged to submit comments on this publication to: Joint Staff J-7, Deputy Director, Joint and Coalition Warfighting, Joint and Coalition Warfighting Center, ATTN: Joint Doctrine Support Division, 116 Lake View Parkway, Suffolk, VA 23435-2697. These comments should address content (accuracy, usefulness, consistency, and organization), writing, and appearance.

2. Authorship

The lead agent and Joint Staff doctrine sponsor for this publication is the Director for Manpower and Personnel (J-1).

3. Supersession

This publication supersedes JP 1-0, 16 October 2006, *Personnel Support to Joint Operations*.

4. Change Recommendations

a. Recommendations for urgent changes to this publication should be submitted:

TO: JOINT STAFF WASHINGTON DC//J7-JEDD//J1//

b. Routine changes should be submitted electronically to the Deputy Director, Joint and Coalition Warfighting, Joint and Coalition Warfighting Center, Joint Doctrine Support Division and info the lead agent and the Director for Joint Force Development, J-7/JEDD.

c. When a Joint Staff directorate submits a proposal to the CJCS that would change source document information reflected in this publication, that directorate will include a proposed change to this publication as an enclosure to its proposal. The Services and other organizations are requested to notify the Joint Staff J-7 when changes to source documents reflected in this publication are initiated.

5. Distribution of Printed Publications

Local reproduction is authorized and access to unclassified publications is unrestricted. However, access to and reproduction authorization for classified JPs must be in accordance with DOD 5200.1-R, *Information Security Program*.

6. Distribution of Electronic Publications

a. Joint Staff J-7 will not print copies of JPs for distribution. Electronic versions are available on JDEIS at https://jdeis.js.mil (NIPRNET), and http://jdeis.js.smil.mil (SIPRNET), and on the JEL at http://www.dtic.mil/doctrine (NIPRNET).

b. Only approved JPs and joint test publications are releasable outside the CCMDs, Services, and Joint Staff. Release of any classified JP to foreign governments or foreign nationals must be requested through the local embassy (Defense Attaché Office) to DIA, Defense Foreign Liaison/IE-3, 200 MacDill Blvd., Joint Base Anacostia-Bolling, Washington, DC 20340-5100.

c. JEL CD-ROM. Upon request of a joint doctrine development community member, the Joint Staff J-7 will produce and deliver one CD-ROM with current JPs. This JEL CD-ROM will be updated not less than semi-annually and when received can be locally reproduced for use within the combatant commands and Services.

GLOSSARY
PART I—ABBREVIATIONS AND ACRONYMS

AAFES	Army and Air Force Exchange Service
AC	Active Component
ACSA	acquisition and cross-servicing agreement
ADSW	active duty for special work
ADUSD(TP)	Assistant Deputy Under Secretary of Defense, Transportation Policy
AFE	Armed Forces Entertainment
AFI	Air Force instruction
AMT	aerial mail terminal
AOR	area of responsibility
APO	Army post office
APOD	aerial port of debarkation
APOE	aerial port of embarkation
AR	Army regulation
ARC	American Red Cross
BAH	basic allowance for housing
BAS	basic allowance for subsistence
BOSS	base operating support service
CA	civil affairs
CAAF	contractor personnel authorized to accompany the force
CAC	common access card
CAP	crisis action planning
CCDR	combatant commander
CCMD	combatant command
CDO	commander, detainee operations
CDRUSEUCOM	Commander, United States European Command
CDRUSNORTHCOM	Commander, United States Northern Command
CDRUSSOCOM	Commander, United States Special Operations Command
CJCS	Chairman of the Joint Chiefs of Staff
CJCSI	Chairman of the Joint Chiefs of Staff instruction
CJCSM	Chairman of the Joint Chiefs of Staff manual
CJTF	commander, joint task force
COA	course of action
CONOPS	concept of operations
CONUS	continental United States
CSA	combat support agency
CSP	career sea pay
CTS	Contingency Tracking System
DA	Department of the Army
DBIDS	Defense Biometric Identification System

DD	Department of Defense (form)
DDSM	Defense Distinguished Service Medal
DEERS	Defense Enrollment Eligibility Reporting System
DFAS	Defense Finance and Accounting Service
DJS	Director, Joint Staff
DMDC	defense manpower data center
DMSM	Defense Meritorious Service Medal
DNA	deoxyribonucleic acid
DOD	Department of Defense
DODD	Department of Defense directive
DODFMR	Department of Defense Financial Management Regulation
DODI	Department of Defense instruction
DOS	Department of State
DOX-T	direct operational exchange–tactical
DPA	danger pay allowance
DSCA	defense support of civil authorities
DSSM	Defense Superior Service Medal
DVD	digital video device
EA	executive agent
EEO	equal employment opportunity
EER	enlisted employee review
e-JMAPS	Electronic Joint Manpower and Personnel System
ESO	Expeditionary Support Organization (DFAS)
FCC	functional combatant commander
FD	from temporary duty
FPD	foreign post differential
FPO	fleet post office
GCC	geographic combatant commander
GFM	Global Force Management
GFMAP	Global Force Management Allocation Plan
GFMB	Global Force Management Board
GFMIG	Global Force Management Implementation Guidance
HFP	hostile fire pay
HIV	human immunodeficiency virus
HN	host nation
HQ	headquarters
HSM	humanitarian service medal
HUMINT	human intelligence
IAW	in accordance with
IDP	imminent danger pay

IGO	intergovernmental organization
J-1	manpower and personnel directorate of a joint staff
J-3	operations directorate of a joint staff
J-4	logistics directorate of a joint staff
J-5	plans directorate of a joint staff
J-6	communications system directorate of a joint staff
J-31	Joint Force Coordinator (Joint Staff)
JAMMS	Joint Asset Movement Management System
JFC	joint force commander
JFHQ	joint force headquarters
JFMC	joint fleet mail center
JFTR	joint Federal travel regulations
JIA	joint individual augmentation
JMD	joint manning document
JMMT	joint military mail terminal
JMP	joint manpower program
JMPA	joint military postal activity
JMUA	Joint Meritorious Unit Award
JOA	joint operations area
JOPES	Joint Operation Planning and Execution System
JP	joint publication
JPARR	joint personnel accountability reconciliation and reporting
JPC	joint postal cell
JPERSTAT	joint personnel status and casualty report
JPOC	joint personnel operations center
JPRC	joint personnel reception center
JPTTA	joint personnel training and tracking activity
JRS	joint reporting structure
JRSOI	joint reception, staging, onward movement, and integration
JSAM	Joint Service Achievement Medal
JSCM	Joint Service Commendation Medal
JTF	joint task force
JTMD	joint table of mobilization and distribution
LCM	letter-class mail
LOA	letter of authorization
LOE	letter of evaluation
MCA	mail control activity
MEO	military equal opportunity
MFE	mobile field exchange
MNF	multinational force
MOA	memorandum of agreement
MOU	memorandum of understanding

MPO	military post office
MPS	Military Postal Service
MPSA	Military Postal Service Agency
MWR	morale, welfare, and recreation
NAF	nonappropriated funds
NATO	North Atlantic Treaty Organization
NDRC	National Detainee Reporting Center
NEO	noncombatant evacuation operation
NGO	nongovernmental organization
NIPRNET	Nonsecure Internet Protocol Router Network
NOK	next of kin
NTS	noncombatant evacuation operations tracking system
OER	officer evaluation report
OPCON	operational control
OPLAN	operation plan
OPR	office of primary responsibility
OPREP	operational report
OPSEC	operations security
OSD	Office of the Secretary of Defense
PARS	Personnel and Accountability System
PDUSD(P&R)	Principal Deputy Under Secretary of Defense (Personnel and Readiness)
PNA	postal net alert
POC	point of contact
POS	point of sale
POV	privately owned vehicle
PR	personnel recovery
PRC	Presidential Reserve Call-up
QHDA	qualified hazardous duty area
R&R	rest and recuperation
RC	Reserve Component
SAPR	sexual assault prevention and response
SARC	sexual assault response coordinator
SecDef	Secretary of Defense
SHAPE	Supreme Headquarters Allied Powers, Europe
SIPRNET	SECRET Internet Protocol Router Network
SITREP	situation report
SLA	special leave accrual
SOF	special operations forces
SPM	service postal manager

SPOD	seaport of debarkation
SPOE	seaport of embarkation
SPOT	Synchronized Predeployment and Operational Tracker
SSPM	single-service postal manager
TAD	temporary additional duty (non-unit-related personnel)
TD	temporary duty
TDRC	theater detainee reporting center
TDY	temporary duty
TOR	term of reference
TPFDD	time-phased force and deployment data
UCMJ	Uniform Code of Military Justice
UCP	Unified Command Plan
UN	United Nations
USACFSC	United States Army Community and Family Support Center
USC	United States Code
USCG	United States Coast Guard
USD(AT&L)	Under Secretary of Defense for Acquisition, Technology, and Logistics
USD(P&R)	Under Secretary of Defense for Personnel and Readiness
USEUCOM	United States European Command
USG	United States Government
USNMR	United States National Military representative
USPS	United States Postal Service
USSOCOM	United States Special Operations Command
USTRANSCOM	United States Transportation Command
VA	victim advocate
WG	working group

PART II—TERMS AND DEFINITIONS

active duty for special work. A tour of active duty for reserve personnel authorized from military and reserve personnel appropriations for work on active or reserve component programs. Also called **ADSW.** (Approved for incorporation into JP 1-02.)

any Service member mail. None. (Approved for removal from JP 1-02.)

Army and Air Force Exchange Service imprest fund activity. None. (Approved for removal from JP 1-02.)

beleaguered. None. (Approved for removal from JP 1-02.)

billet. None. (Approved for removal from JP 1-02.)

captured. None. (Approved for removal from JP 1-02.)

combat readiness. Synonymous with operational readiness, with respect to missions or functions performed in combat. (Approved for incorporation into JP 1-02 with JP 1-0 as the source JP.)

contingency ZIP Code. A ZIP Code consisting of a five-digit base with a four-digit add-on to assist in routing and sorting assigned by Military Postal Service Agency to a contingency post office for the tactical use of the Armed Forces on a temporary basis. (Approved for incorporation into JP 1-02.)

critical joint duty assignment billet. A joint duty assignment position for which, considering the duties and responsibilities of the position, it is highly important that the assigned officer be particularly trained in, and oriented toward, joint matters. (Approved for incorporation into JP 1-02.)

data element. 1. A basic unit of information built on standard structures having a unique meaning and distinct units or values. 2. In electronic recordkeeping, a combination of characters or bytes referring to one separate item of information, such as name, address, or age. (Approved for incorporation into JP 1-02 with JP 1-0 as the source JP.)

defense sexual assault incident database. A Department of Defense database that captures and serves as the reporting source for all sexual assault data collected by the Services. Also called **DSAID.** (Approved for inclusion in JP 1-02.)

Department of Defense civilian. A Federal civilian employee of the Department of Defense directly hired and paid from appropriated or nonappropriated funds, under permanent or temporary appointment. (Approved for incorporation into JP 1-02.)

detained. None. (Approved for removal from JP 1-02.)

emergency-essential employee. A Department of Defense civilian employee whose assigned duties and responsibilities must be accomplished following the evacuation of non-essential personnel (including dependents) during a declared emergency or outbreak of war. (Approved for incorporation into JP 1-02.)

filler personnel. None. (Approved for removal from JP 1-02.)

flag officer. None. (Approved for removal from JP 1-02.)

force list. None. (Approved for removal from JP 1-02.)

foreign national. Any person other than a US citizen, US permanent or temporary legal resident alien, or person in US custody. (Approved for incorporation into JP 1-02 with JP 1-0 as the source JP.)

free mail. Correspondence of a personal nature that weighs less than 11 ounces, to include audio and video recording tapes, from a member of the Armed Forces or designated civilian, mailed postage free from a Secretary of Defense approved free mail zone. (JP 1-02. SOURCE: JP 1-0)

imprest fund. A cash fund of a fixed amount established through an advance of funds, without appropriation change, to an authorized imprest fund cashier to effect immediate cash payments of relatively small amounts for authorized purchases of supplies and nonpersonal services. (Approved for incorporation into JP 1-02 with JP 1-0 as the source JP.)

imprest funds. None. (Approved form removal from JP 1-02.)

individual sponsored dependent. None. (Approved for removal from JP 1-02.)

interned. None. (Approved for removal from JP 1-02.)

inter-Service training. None. (Approved for removal from JP 1-02.)

joint manpower program. The policy, processes, and systems used in determination and prioritization within and among joint Service manpower requirements. Also called **JMP.** (Approved for incorporation into JP 1-02.)

joint personnel accountability reconciliation and reporting. A data repository developed and implemented by the Defense Manpower Data Center that consumes and reconciles data from existing Service deployment systems. Also called **JPARR.** (Approved for inclusion in JP 1-02.)

joint personnel training and tracking activity. The continental United States center established to facilitate the reception, accountability, processing, training, and onward movement of individual augmentees preparing for overseas movement to support a joint military operation. Also called **JPTTA.** (Approved for incorporation into JP 1-02.)

joint personnel reception center. A center established in an operational area by the appropriate joint force commander with the responsibility for the in-processing and out-processing of personnel upon their arrival in and departure from the theater. Also called **JPRC.** (Approved for inclusion in JP 1-02.)

joint reception center. None. (Approved for removal from JP 1-02.)

joint specialty officer or joint specialist. None. (Approved for removal from JP 1-02.)

joint table of distribution. A manpower document that identifies the positions and enumerates the spaces that have been approved for each organizational element of a joint activity for a specific fiscal year (authorization year), and those accepted for the four subsequent fiscal years (program years). Also called **JTD.** (Approved for incorporation into JP 1-02.)

key position. A civilian position, public or private (designated by the employer and approved by the Secretary concerned), that cannot be vacated during war or national emergency. (Approved for incorporation into JP 1-02 with JP 1-0 as the source JP.)

mail embargo. A temporary shutdown or redirection of mail flow to or from a specific location. (JP 1-02. SOURCE: JP 1-0)

manpower. None. (Approved for removal from JP 1-02.)

manpower management. The means of manpower control to ensure the most efficient and economical use of available manpower. (Approved for inclusion in JP 1-02.)

manpower requirements. Human resources needed to accomplish specified work loads of organizations. (Approved for incorporation into JP 1-02 with JP 1-0 as the source JP.)

manpower resources. None. (Approved for removal from JP 1-02.)

maximum enlisted amount. None. (Approved for removal from JP 1-02.)

military post office. A branch of a designated US-based post office established by US Postal Service authority and operated by one of the Services. Also called **MPO.** (Approved for incorporation into JP 1-02.)

Military Postal Service. The command, organization, personnel, and facilities established to provide a means for the transmission of mail to and from the Department of Defense, members of the US Armed Forces, and other authorized agencies and individuals. Also called **MPS.** (Approved for incorporation into JP 1-02.)

Military Postal Service Agency. The single manager operating agency established to manage the Military Postal Service. Also called **MPSA.** (Approved for incorporation into JP 1-02 with JP 1-0 as the source JP.)

missing. None. (Approved for removal from JP 1-02.)

missing in action. None. (Approved for removal from JP 1-02.)

morale, welfare, and recreation. The merging of multiple unconnected disciplines into programs which improve unit readiness, promote fitness, build unit morale and cohesion, enhance quality of life, and provide recreational, social, and other support services. Also called **MWR.** (Approved for inclusion in JP 1-02.)

nonappropriated funds. Funds generated by Department of Defense personnel and their dependents used to augment funds appropriated by the Congress to provide a comprehensive, morale-building welfare, religious, educational, and recreational programs. Also called **NAF.** (Approved for incorporation into JP 1-02.)

non-unit-related personnel. All personnel requiring transportation to or from an operational area, other than those assigned to a specific unit. Also called **NRP** or **NUP.** (Approved for incorporation into JP 1-02.)

operational readiness. The capability of a unit/formation, ship, weapon system, or equipment to perform the missions or functions for which it is organized or designed. Also called **OR.** (Approved for incorporation into JP 1-02.)

personnel. Those individuals required in either a military or civilian capacity to accomplish the assigned mission. (Approved for incorporation into JP 1-02 with JP 1-0 as the source JP.)

personnel accountability. The process of identifying, capturing, and recording the personal identification information of an individual usually through the use of a database. (Approved for inclusion in JP 1-02.)

personnel replacement center. None. (Approved for removal from JP 1-02.)

personnel services support. Service-provided sustainment activities that support a Service member during both joint exercises and joint operations. Also called **PSS.** (Approved for inclusion in JP 1-02.)

reclama. None. (Approved for removal from JP 1-02.)

repatriation. 1. The procedure whereby American citizens and their families are officially processed back into the United States subsequent to an evacuation. (JP 3-68) 2. The release and return of enemy prisoners of war to their own country in accordance with the 1949 Geneva Convention Relative to the Treatment of Prisoners of War. (JP 1-02. SOURCE: JP 1-0)

replacements. None. (Approved for removal from JP 1-02.)

rest and recuperation. The withdrawal of individuals from combat or duty in a combat area for short periods of rest and recuperation. Also called **R&R.** (Approved for incorporation into JP 1-02 with JP 1-0 as the source JP.)

restricted reporting. Reporting option that allows sexual assault victims to confidentially disclose the assault to specified individual and receive medical treatment without triggering an official investigation. (Approved for inclusion in JP 1-02.)

security clearance. An administrative determination by competent authority that an individual is eligible for access to classified information. (Approved for incorporation into JP 1-02.)

sexual assault forensic examination kit. The medical and forensic examination kit used to ensure controlled procedures and safekeeping of any bodily specimens in a sexual assault case. Also called **SAFE kit.** (Approved for inclusion in JP 1-02.)

sexual assault prevention and response program. A Department of Defense program for the Military Departments and Department of Defense components that establishes sexual assault prevention and response policies to be implemented worldwide. Also called **SAPR program.** (Approved for inclusion in JP 1-02.)

sexual assault response coordinator. The single point of contact at an installation or within a geographic area who overseas sexual assault awareness, prevention, and response. Also called **SARC.** (Approved for inclusion in JP 1-02.)

single-service manager. A Service component commander who is assigned the responsibility and delegated the authority to coordinate and/or perform specified personnel support or personnel service support functions in the theater of operations. (Approved for incorporation into JP 1-02.)

space available mail. None. (Approved for removal from JP 1-02.)

sponsor. None. (Approved for removal from JP 1-02.)

staff. None. (Approved for removal from JP 1-02.)

staff supervision. None. (Approved for removal from JP 1-02.)

training period. None. (Approved for removal from JP 1-02.)

uniformed services. The Army, Navy, Air Force, Marine Corps, Coast Guard, National Oceanic and Atmospheric Administration, and Public Health Services. (Approved for incorporation into JP 1-02 with JP 1-0 as the source JP.)

unit identification code. A six-character, alphanumeric code that uniquely identifies each Active, Reserve, and National Guard unit of the Armed Forces. Also called **UIC.** (Approved for incorporation into JP 1-02 with JP 1-0 as the source JP.)

Universal Postal Union. None. (Approved for removal from JP 1-02.)

unrestricted reporting. A process that a Service member uses to disclose, without requesting confidentiality or restricted reporting, that he or she is the victim of a sexual assault. (Approved for inclusion in JP 1-02.)

voluntary training. None. (Approved for removal from JP 1-02.)

voluntary training unit. None. (Approved for removal from JP 1-02.)

Intentionally Blank

JOINT DOCTRINE PUBLICATIONS HIERARCHY

```
                          ┌─────────────┐
                          │    JP 1     │
                          │   JOINT     │
                          │  DOCTRINE   │
                          └─────────────┘
```

JP 1-0	JP 2-0	JP 3-0	JP 4-0	JP 5-0	JP 6-0
PERSONNEL	INTELLIGENCE	OPERATIONS	LOGISTICS	PLANS	COMMUNICATIONS SYSTEM

All joint publications are organized into a comprehensive hierarchy as shown in the chart above. **Joint Publication (JP) 1-0** is in the **Personnel** series of joint doctrine publications. The diagram below illustrates an overview of the development process:

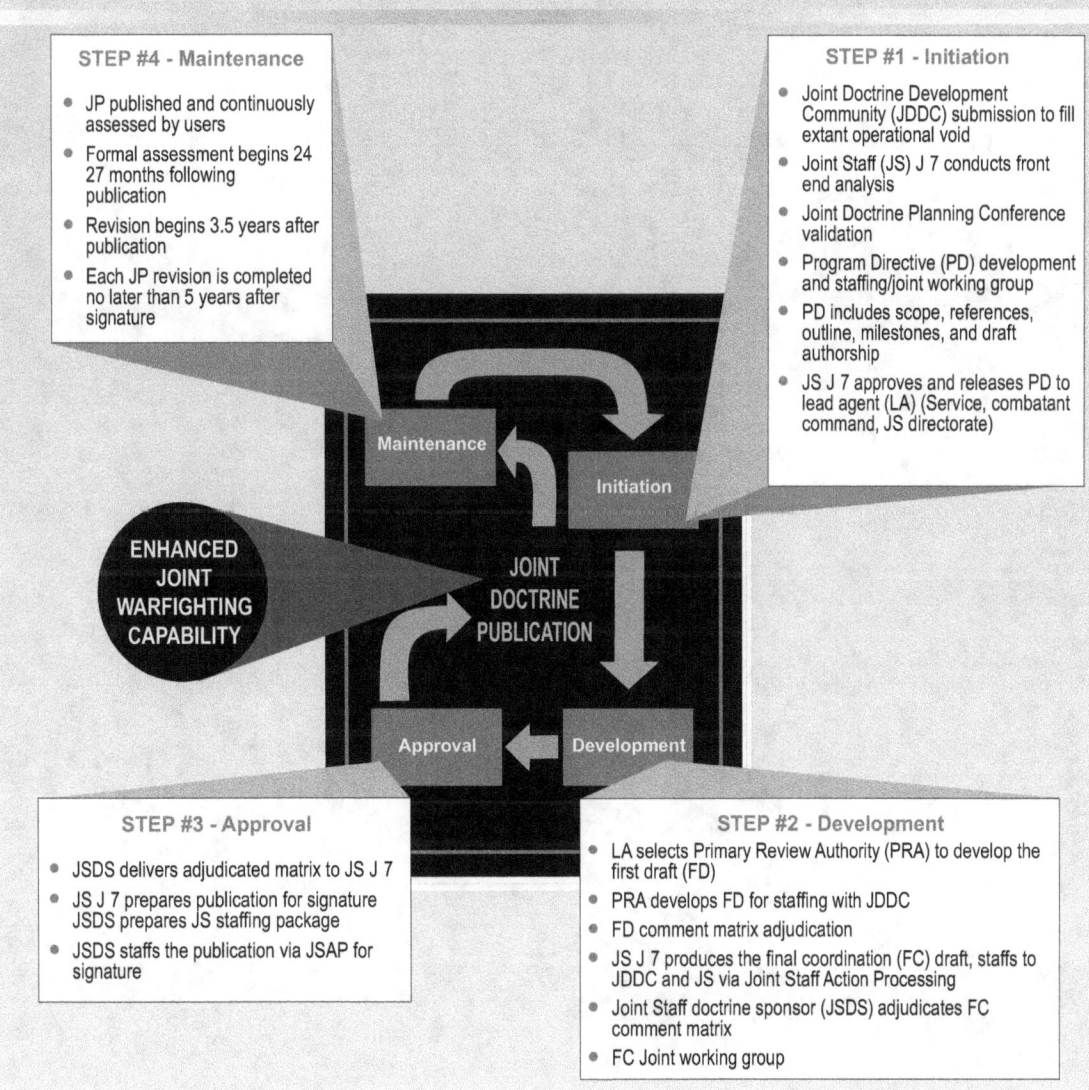

STEP #4 - Maintenance

- JP published and continuously assessed by users
- Formal assessment begins 24 27 months following publication
- Revision begins 3.5 years after publication
- Each JP revision is completed no later than 5 years after signature

STEP #1 - Initiation

- Joint Doctrine Development Community (JDDC) submission to fill extant operational void
- Joint Staff (JS) J 7 conducts front end analysis
- Joint Doctrine Planning Conference validation
- Program Directive (PD) development and staffing/joint working group
- PD includes scope, references, outline, milestones, and draft authorship
- JS J 7 approves and releases PD to lead agent (LA) (Service, combatant command, JS directorate)

ENHANCED JOINT WARFIGHTING CAPABILITY

Maintenance — Initiation — JOINT DOCTRINE PUBLICATION — Development — Approval

STEP #3 - Approval

- JSDS delivers adjudicated matrix to JS J 7
- JS J 7 prepares publication for signature JSDS prepares JS staffing package
- JSDS staffs the publication via JSAP for signature

STEP #2 - Development

- LA selects Primary Review Authority (PRA) to develop the first draft (FD)
- PRA develops FD for staffing with JDDC
- FD comment matrix adjudication
- JS J 7 produces the final coordination (FC) draft, staffs to JDDC and JS via Joint Staff Action Processing
- Joint Staff doctrine sponsor (JSDS) adjudicates FC comment matrix
- FC Joint working group

www.ingramcontent.com/pod-product-compliance
Lightning Source LLC
Chambersburg PA
CBHW081325310526
45789CB00018B/2370